To the Bad Step, Give Haste.

Santos Omar Medrano Chura

Published by Santos Omar Medrano Chura, 2023.

TO THE BAD STEP, GIVE HASTE.

First edition. November 14, 2023.

ISBN: 979-8223029304

Written by Santos Omar Medrano Chura.

To the Bad Step, Give Haste.

How to overcome life's obstacles with optimism and resilience.

Author: Santos Omar Medrano Chura

Terms and Conditions

To the bad step give haste
How to overcome life's obstacles with optimism and resilience.

Introduction.

Have you ever felt overwhelmed by life's difficulties? Have you felt discouraged, frustrated or helpless in the face of obstacles? Have you wondered how to overcome problems with optimism and resilience?

If your answer is yes, this book is for you. In it, you will find practical advice, inspiring examples and simple exercises that will help you face adversity with a positive attitude and find the opportunities in every challenge.

The title of this book, "al mal paso darle prisa", is a popular saying that means to act quickly and decisively in difficult situations, without being overcome by fear or despair. It is an invitation to take control of your life, to take responsibility for your actions and to seek creative and effective solutions.

This book is divided into ten chapters, each dedicated to a key aspect of overcoming life's obstacles with optimism and resilience. In each chapter, you will learn how to:

Have a clear vision and purpose to guide and motivate you.

Develop confidence in yourself and your abilities.

Manage stress, anxiety and fear that paralyze or block you.

Cultivate gratitude, joy and humor that fill you with energy and hope.

Communicate effectively and create positive relationships that support and enrich you.

Learn from mistakes and failures that make you grow and improve.

Adapt to the change and uncertainty that challenges and drives you.

Tap into your creativity and passion that differentiates and fulfills you.

Set realistic and achievable goals that will guide you and bring you closer to your dreams.

Celebrate your accomplishments and recognize your strengths that empower and value you.

This book does not pretend to be a magic recipe or a definitive solution to all your problems. Nor does it pretend to be a self-help manual or a treatise on psychology. This book is simply a traveling companion, a friend who listens to you, understands you and encourages you. A friend who tells you: to the bad step hurry, to the good step too. Because life is a wonderful adventure, but also full of surprises, difficulties and opportunities. And you are the protagonist, the hero or heroine of your own story.

So don't wait any longer. Open this book and start hurrying the bad step. And remember: there is always a light at the end of the tunnel, there is always a way out, there is always hope. And there is always someone who believes in you. I believe in you. Do you? Do you believe in yourself?

1. The importance of having a clear vision and purpose.

What moves you, what inspires you, what you are passionate about? What do you want to achieve in your life and why? What makes you get up every morning with enthusiasm and energy? What gives meaning to your existence?

These are some of the questions that will help you discover your vision and purpose. Your vision is the mental image you have of your ideal future, of what you want your life to be like in all aspects: personal, professional, family, social, spiritual, etc. Your purpose is the raison d'être of your vision, the reason for your dreams, the why of your goals.

Having a clear vision and purpose is fundamental to overcome life's obstacles with optimism and resilience. Because when you have a clear vision and purpose, you know where you are going and why you are going. You know what your destination is and what your path is. You know what your north is and what your compass is.

When you have a clear vision and purpose, you have a guide, a direction, an orientation. You have a focus, a motivation, an inspiration. You have a challenge, an opportunity, an illusion.

When you have a clear vision and purpose, obstacles become challenges, difficulties become learnings, problems become solutions. When you have a clear vision and purpose, you don't give up in the face of adversity, but face it with determination and confidence. When you have a clear vision and purpose, you don't settle for what you have, you seek what you want.

But how can you define your vision and purpose? How can you know what you want to achieve in your life and why? How can you create your ideal future and your reason for being?

To do so, I propose three steps:

What do you want to achieve in your life and why?

How to define your mission, vision and values.

How to align your actions with your purpose.

Let's look at each of them in more detail.

- What do you want to achieve in your life and why?

The first step in defining your vision and purpose is to ask yourself what you want to achieve in your life and why. That is, what are your dreams, your aspirations, your desires. And also what are the reasons that drive you to pursue them, the benefits they bring you, the feelings they generate.

To answer these questions, you can do the following exercise:

Take a sheet of paper and a pen.

Write in the center of the sheet the question: What do I want to achieve in my life?

Around the question, write all the answers you can think of, without censoring or limiting yourself. You can write single words or short phrases. You can use different colors or drawings to represent your ideas.

When you have finished writing all your answers, review what you have written and choose the three most important to you. The three that most excite, excite or inspire you.

For each of the three answers chosen, write below the question: Why do I want to achieve this?

Write down as many reasons as you can think of for each answer. You can think about how you would feel if you achieved that, what benefits you would have, what impact it would have on you or others.

When you have finished writing all your reasons, review what you have written and choose the one that is most important to you. The most powerful, the most meaningful or the most profound.

At the end of this exercise, you will have three answers to the question: What do I want to achieve in my life? And three reasons to the question: Why do I want to achieve this? These will be the basis of your vision and purpose.

For example, suppose your three answers to the question: What do I want to achieve in my life? are:

To be happy.

Helping others.

Traveling the world.

And let's assume that your three reasons to the question: Why do I want to achieve this? are:

Being happy: Because it is what makes me feel full and fulfilled.

Helping others: Because it is what makes me feel useful and generous.

Traveling the world: Because it's what makes me feel free and curious.

These would be the basis of your vision and purpose. From them, you could define your mission, your vision and your values.

- How to define your mission, vision and values.

The second step in defining your vision and purpose is to define your mission, vision and values. These are three concepts that will help you give shape and meaning to your dreams and your reasons.

Your mission is your purpose statement, the reason for your existence, the raison d'être of your life. It is the answer to the question: What am I here for? Your mission expresses the impact you want to have on the world, the contribution you want to make, the legacy you want to leave.

Your vision is the description of your ideal future, the way you want your life to be, the destination you want to reach. It is the answer to the question: How do I want to live? Your vision expresses the result you want to achieve, the goal you want to reach, the dream you want to fulfill.

Your values are the principles that guide your behavior, what you care about, how you want to act. They are the answer to the question:

What defines me? Your values express the qualities that characterize you, the beliefs that sustain you, the norms that regulate you.

To define your mission, your vision and your values, you can use the bases you obtained in the previous step. That is, the answers to the questions: What do I want to achieve in my life? And Why do I want to achieve this?

To define your mission, you can combine your three reasons into a single sentence that summarizes your purpose. For example:

My mission is to feel full, useful and free.

To define your vision, you can combine your three answers into a single sentence that describes your ideal future. For example:

My vision is to be happy, help others and travel the world.

To define your values, you can choose three words that represent the principles that guide you. For example:

My values are: fullness, generosity and freedom.

At the end of this step, you will have defined your mission, your vision and your values. These will be the pillars of your vision and purpose.

- How to align your actions with your purpose.

The third and final step in defining your vision and purpose is to align your actions with your purpose. That is, make what you do align with what you want and who you are. Make your life consistent with your mission, your vision and your values.

To align your actions with your purpose, you can do the following exercise:

Take a sheet of paper and a pen.

Divide the sheet into four equal parts.

In each part, write one of the following headings: Mission, Vision, Values and Actions.

In the Mission part, write the phrase you defined in the previous step as your purpose statement.

In the Vision section, write the phrase you defined in the previous step as your ideal future description.

In the Values part, write the three words you chose in the previous step as your guiding principles.

In the Actions section, write down all the actions you take or could take to fulfill your mission, achieve your vision and live according to your values. You can think of actions related to all areas of your life: personal, professional, family, social, spiritual, etc.

When you have finished writing down all your actions, review what you have written and evaluate if there is congruence between what you do and what you want and are. Ask yourself if your actions bring you closer or:

They take you away from your mission, your vision and your values.

They make you feel full, useful and free or they make you feel empty, useless and trapped.

They either bring you happiness, help and travel or they bring you unhappiness, selfishness and stagnation.

If you find that there is congruence between your actions and your purpose, congratulate yourself for it and keep it up. If you find that there is incongruence between your actions and your purpose, don't be discouraged or blame yourself for it. Simply recognize what you can improve and make the necessary changes.

To make the necessary changes, you can use the SMART method, which will help you define specific, measurable, achievable, relevant and time-bound actions. For example:

Specific action: I want to write a book on how to overcome life's obstacles with optimism and resilience.

Measurable action: I want to write 10 chapters of 10 pages each.

Achievable action: I want to write the book in 6 months.

Relevant action: I want to write the book because it is my dream, because it makes me happy, because it helps others and because it allows me to travel the world.

Time action: I want to write the book between January 1 and June 30 next year.

At the end of this exercise, you will have aligned your actions with your purpose. These will be the manifestations of your vision and purpose.

In this chapter, we have seen the importance of having a clear vision and purpose. We have seen that having a clear vision and purpose helps us to overcome life's obstacles with optimism and resilience. We have seen that having a clear vision and purpose gives us a guide, a direction, an orientation. We have seen that having a clear vision and purpose gives us a focus, a motivation, an inspiration. We have seen that having a clear vision and purpose gives us a challenge, an opportunity, an illusion.

We have also seen how to define our vision and purpose. We have seen how to ask ourselves what we want to achieve in our life and why. We have seen how to define our mission, our vision and our values. We have seen how to align our actions with our purpose.

I hope you found this chapter useful and interesting. I hope it has helped you discover or clarify your vision and purpose. I hope it has encouraged you to hurry up the wrong step and the right step.

In the next chapter, we will see how to develop confidence in ourselves and our capabilities. We will see how to change our limiting beliefs for empowering beliefs. We will see how to strengthen our self-esteem and self-efficacy.

But before moving on to the next chapter, I invite you to do a brief reflection exercise. I invite you to answer these questions:

What have you learned in this chapter?

What did you like most about this chapter?

What will you apply from this chapter in your life?

Write your answers on a piece of paper or in a journal. Share them with someone if you want to. And above all, put them into practice.

Remember: to the bad step give haste, to the good step also.

See you in the next chapter.

Suggestion:

Take time to reflect on what you want to achieve in your life and why. Don't get carried away by what others expect of you or what society imposes on you. Look for what makes you happy, what you are passionate about, what fulfills you.

Write down your vision and purpose on paper or in a journal. Do it clearly, in detail, with emotion. Use positive, affirmative, powerful words. Read your vision and purpose every day and visualize them in your mind.

Define your mission, your vision and your values. Your mission is your statement of purpose, your reason for being. Your vision is your description of your ideal future, your destiny. Your values are your principles that guide your behavior, your way of being.

Align your actions with your purpose. Make what you do align with what you want and who you are. Make your life consistent with your mission, your vision and your values.

Use the SMART method to define your actions. Make your actions specific, measurable, achievable, relevant and time-bound. This way you will be able to plan, execute and evaluate your actions effectively.

Be flexible and adaptable. Don't stick to a rigid plan or a fixed idea. Accept that change and uncertainty are part of life and can bring new opportunities and learning. Adapt your vision and purpose to the circumstances without losing sight of your essence.

Seek the support of others. Don't try to achieve your vision and purpose alone. Surround yourself with people who share your dreams, your values, your goals. People who support you, encourage you, help you. People who give you feedback, advice, guidance.

Be inspired by other people. Look for references, models, examples of people who have achieved their vision and purpose or are on their way to doing so. People who inspire you, motivate you, teach you. People you admire, respect, love.

Celebrate your progress and recognize your achievements. Don't wait until you reach the end to feel proud of yourself. Recognize every step you take, every action you take, every result you achieve. Reward your efforts, your sacrifices, your successes.

Enjoy the process and the present. Don't obsess about the future or the end result. Enjoy the journey, the learning, the growth. Enjoy the here and now, the moment, the experience.

Conclusion:

These are ten tips to have a clear vision and purpose. I hope you liked them and that you put them into practice.

Remember: having a clear vision and purpose is fundamental to overcome life's obstacles with optimism and resilience.

Remember: to the bad step give haste, to the good step also.

2. How to develop confidence in yourself and your abilities.

Do you feel sure of yourself? Do you believe in yourself and your abilities? Do you value and respect yourself? Do you dare to do what you want and be who you are?

If your answer is yes, congratulations. You are a person with confidence in yourself and your abilities. You are a person with self-esteem and self-efficacy. You are a person who loves, accepts and empowers yourself.

If your answer is no, don't worry. You are not the only one. Many people suffer from lack of confidence in themselves and their abilities. Many people suffer from low self-esteem and low self-efficacy. Many people criticize, reject and limit themselves.

But the good news is that confidence in yourself and your abilities is not something fixed or immutable. It is not something you either have or don't have. It is not something that depends on external or uncontrollable factors. Confidence in yourself and your abilities is something that can be developed, improved and strengthened.

Confidence in yourself and your abilities is the belief you have about your value, your competence and your ability to achieve what you set out to do. It is the attitude you have towards yourself, your possibilities and your challenges. It is the feeling you have of security, respect and love for yourself.

Confidence in yourself and in your abilities is essential to overcome life's obstacles with optimism and resilience. Because when you have confidence in yourself and in your abilities, you feel capable of facing difficulties, of learning from mistakes, of looking for solutions. When you have confidence in yourself and in your abilities, you feel worthy of achieving your goals, of enjoying your successes, of celebrating your achievements. When you have confidence in yourself and your abilities, you feel happy, satisfied and fulfilled.

But how can you develop confidence in yourself and your abilities? How can you believe more in yourself and your possibilities? How can you love yourself more, accept yourself more and empower yourself more?

To do so, I propose three steps:

What limiting beliefs are holding you back?

How to change your internal dialogue and self-image.

How to strengthen your self-esteem and self-efficacy.

Let's look at each of them in more detail.

- What limiting beliefs are holding you back?

The first step in developing confidence in yourself and your abilities is to identify what limiting beliefs are holding you back. Limiting beliefs are those negative ideas or thoughts you have about yourself, your capabilities or the world. They are those phrases that begin with "I can't", "I am not", "I don't have", "I don't deserve", "I don't know", etc.

Limiting beliefs are like invisible chains that tie you down, slow you down, block you. They are like distorted filters that make you see reality in a biased, incomplete or erroneous way. They are like mental viruses that infect you, weaken you, make you sick.

Limiting beliefs can have their origin in diverse sources: past experiences, messages received, social comparisons, irrational fears, etc. But what is important is not so much their origin but their effect: limiting beliefs affect your confidence in yourself and your abilities, your self-esteem and your self-efficacy.

To identify your limiting beliefs, you can do the following exercise:

Take a sheet of paper and a pen.

Write in the center of the sheet the question: What limiting beliefs do I have?

Around the question, write all the answers you can think of, without censoring or limiting yourself. You can write single words or short phrases. You can use different colors or drawings to represent your ideas.

When you have finished writing all your answers, review what you have written and choose the three most important to you. The three that affect you the most, bother you the most, or prevent you from moving forward.

For each of the three answers chosen, write below the question: What evidence do I have that this belief is true?

Write down as much evidence as you can think of for each answer. You can think of facts, data, evidence, testimonies, etc. that support your belief.

When you have finished writing all your evidence, review what you have written and evaluate if it is sufficient, valid and current. Ask yourself if there are other evidences that contradict your belief, if there are other ways to interpret reality, if there are other possibilities to act.

At the end of this exercise, you will have identified your limiting beliefs and their evidence. These will be the barriers that you will have to overcome to develop your confidence in yourself and your capabilities.

For example, suppose your three limiting beliefs are:

I can't write a book.

I'm not smart enough.

I don't have time to do what I want to do.

And suppose your evidence is:

I can't write a book: Because I've never written anything, because I don't know what to write about, because no one will read me.

I am not smart enough: Because I got bad grades in school, because I find it hard to understand things, because I compare myself with people more prepared than me.

I don't have time to do what I want to do: Because I have too many obligations, because I don't know how to organize myself, because unforeseen events always arise.

These would be your limiting beliefs and their evidence. But are they sufficient, valid and current? Is there other evidence that contradicts your beliefs? Are there other ways to interpret reality? Are there other possibilities to act?

Here are some examples:

I cannot write a book: Is it true that you have never written anything? Have you not written letters, emails, messages, diaries, etc.? Is it true that you do not know what to write about? Do you not have any passion, any knowledge, any experience that you can share? Is it true that nobody will read you? Are there no people interested in your subject, your style, your message?

I'm not smart enough: Is it true that you got bad grades in school? Wasn't there a subject or activity that you excelled in or enjoyed? Is it true that you have trouble understanding things? Isn't there a way to learn that is better suited to you or your pace? Is it true that you compare yourself to people who are better prepared than you? Aren't there people who are less prepared than you or with whom you can collaborate?

I don't have time to do what I want to do: Is it true that you have many obligations? Can't you delegate some of them or negotiate their priority or deadline? Is it true that you don't know how to organize yourself? Can't you use some tool or method to help you plan and manage your time? Is it true that unforeseen events always come up? Can't you anticipate some of them or reserve some space for them?

As you can see, there is other evidence that contradicts your limiting beliefs. There are other ways to interpret reality. There are other possibilities to act. You just have to look for them and find them.

- How to change your internal dialogue and self-image.

The second step in developing confidence in yourself and your abilities is to change your internal dialogue and self-image. The internal dialogue is the conversation you have with yourself. Self-image is the mental image you have of yourself.

Your internal dialogue and self-image directly influence your self-confidence and capabilities:

Because what you say to yourself and what you show affects what you feel and what you do. Because what you feel and what you do affects what you achieve and who you are.

If your internal dialogue and self-image are negative, you will feel insecure, incompetent and incapable. You will behave in a passive, avoidant or defeatist manner. You will achieve little or nothing. You will be a person with low confidence in yourself and your abilities.

If your internal dialogue and self-image are positive, you will feel confident, competent and capable. You will behave actively, assertively or proactively. You will accomplish much or everything. You will be a person with high confidence in yourself and your abilities.

Therefore, it is important that you change your internal dialogue and your self-image if they are negative. Transform them into positive ones. Turn them into your allies and not your enemies.

To change your internal dialogue and your self-image, you can do the following exercise:

Take a sheet of paper and a pen.

Divide the sheet into two equal parts.

In one part, write the title: Negative Internal Dialogue. In the other part, write the title: Positive Internal Dialogue.

In the Negative Internal Dialogue part, write down all the negative phrases you say to yourself. You can use the limiting beliefs you identified in the previous step or add new ones. For example: I can't write a book. I am not smart enough. I don't have time to do what I want to do.

In the Positive Internal Dialogue part, write down all the positive phrases that you could say to yourself. You can use the evidence that contradicts your limiting beliefs or add new ones. For example: I can write a book if I put my mind to it. I am smart and can learn whatever

I am interested in. I have time to do what I want to do if I organize myself well.

When you have finished writing all your sentences, review what you have written and choose the three most important to you. The three that most affect you, help you or drive you.

For each of the three phrases chosen, write below an example of a situation in which you could use it. You can think of a real or imaginary situation, past, present or future. For example: I can write a book if I put my mind to it. Example: When I sit down at the computer and start writing the first chapter of my book.

When you have finished writing all your examples, review what you have written and practice saying the positive phrases out loud or mentally. Do it with conviction, with emotion, with force.

Repeat this exercise every time you catch yourself saying negative phrases. Replace them with positive phrases. Do this until it becomes a habit.

At the end of this exercise, you will have changed your negative internal dialogue for a positive one. This will be the first step in changing your negative self-image to a positive one.

To change your negative self-image to a positive one, you can do the following exercise:

Take a sheet of paper and a pen.

Draw a large circle in the center of the sheet.

Inside the circle, draw or write how you see yourself now. You can use words, pictures, symbols, colors, etc. to represent your current self-image. For example: A sad face, broken glasses, one word: failure.

Outside the circle, draw or write how you would like to see yourself in the future. You can use words, pictures, symbols, colors, etc. to represent your ideal self-image. For example: A smiling face, new glasses, one word: success.

When you have finished drawing or writing your current self-image and your ideal self-image, review what you have done and choose the three most important differences between the two. The three that most stand out to you, make you uncomfortable, or motivate you.

For each of the three differences chosen, write below an action you could take to reduce or eliminate that difference. You can think of a concrete, simple and feasible action that will bring you closer to your ideal self-image. For example: Difference: A sad face vs. a smiling face. Action: Smile more often and look for reasons to laugh.

When you have finished writing down all your actions, review what you have written and practice doing those actions in your daily life. Do it often, with perseverance, with enthusiasm.

Repeat this exercise every time you catch yourself seeing yourself in a negative way. Replace your negative self-image with a positive one. Do this until it becomes a habit.

At the end of this exercise, you will have changed your negative self-image into a positive one. This will be the second step in developing your confidence in yourself and your abilities.

- How to strengthen your self-esteem and self-efficacy.

The third and final step in developing confidence in yourself and your abilities is to strengthen your self-esteem and self-efficacy. Self-esteem is the appreciation or value you have for yourself. Self-efficacy is the belief or confidence you have in your ability to achieve what you set out to do.

Self-esteem and self-efficacy are two essential components of confidence in yourself and your abilities. Because when you have high self-esteem, you love, accept and respect yourself. When you have high self-efficacy, you believe in yourself, in your possibilities and in your resources.

Self-esteem and self-efficacy are mutually reinforcing. When you have high self-esteem, you feel capable of meeting challenges and achieving goals. When you have high self-efficacy, you achieve the results you want and feel satisfied and proud.

But how can you strengthen your self-esteem and self-efficacy? How can you love yourself more, accept yourself more and respect yourself more? How can you believe more in yourself, in your possibilities and in your resources?

To do so, I propose three steps:

Change your internal dialogue and your self-image.

Recognize your accomplishments and strengths.

Tackle challenges and seek learning.

Let's look at each of them in more detail.

Change your internal dialogue and your self-image.

The first step to strengthen your self-esteem and self-efficacy is to change your internal dialogue and self-image. We have already seen this step in the previous section, so we are not going to repeat it here. We will only remind you of its importance.

Changing your internal dialogue and self-image is fundamental to strengthening your self-esteem and self-efficacy. Because what you say to yourself and what you show yourself affects what you feel and what you do. Because what you feel and what you do affects what you achieve and who you are.

If you change your internal dialogue and your self-image from negative to positive, you will also change your feelings, your behaviors, your results and your identity. You will feel more confident, competent and capable. You will behave more actively, assertively or proactively. You will achieve more or everything. You will be a person with high confidence in yourself and your abilities.

So remember: change your internal dialogue and self-image from negative to positive.

Recognize your accomplishments and strengths.

The second step to strengthening your self-esteem and self-efficacy is to recognize your accomplishments and strengths:

Your achievements are the results you have obtained thanks to your effort, your dedication, your talent. Your strengths are the qualities that characterize you, the skills you possess, the resources you have.

Recognizing your achievements and strengths is important to strengthen your self-esteem and self-efficacy. Because when you recognize your accomplishments and your strengths, you realize what you are worth, what you can do, what you have. You realize that you are a valuable, capable and gifted person.

Recognizing your achievements and strengths makes you feel proud of yourself, your work, your career. It makes you feel satisfied with what you have done, what you have learned, what you have grown. It makes you feel happy, fulfilled and fulfilled.

Recognizing your achievements and strengths motivates you to keep moving forward, to keep improving, to keep enjoying. It motivates you to set yourself new challenges, to seek new opportunities, to live new experiences. It motivates you to continue living with passion, with illusion, with purpose.

To recognize your achievements and strengths, you can do the following exercise:

Take a sheet of paper and a pen.

Divide the sheet into two equal parts.

In one part, write the title: Achievements. In the other part, write the title: Strengths.

In the Achievements section, write down all the results you have achieved in your life thanks to your effort, your dedication, your talent. You can think of results related to all areas of your life: personal, professional, family, social, spiritual, etc. For example: I have written a book. I have finished a career. I have started a family.

In the Strengths section, write down all the qualities that characterize you, the skills you possess, the resources you have. You can think of qualities related to all aspects of your person: physical, mental, emotional, social, spiritual, etc. For example: I am creative. I am intelligent. I am generous.

When you have finished writing down all your accomplishments and strengths, review what you have written and choose the three most important to you. The three that most represent, define or distinguish you.

For each of the three achievements and strengths chosen, write below an example of how you have demonstrated or used them in your life. You can think of a real or imaginary example, past, present or future. For example: I am creative. Example: I have written a book about overcoming life's obstacles with optimism and resilience.

When you have finished writing all your examples, review what you have written and practice telling yourself the accomplishments and strengths out loud or mentally. Do it with conviction, with emotion, with strength.

Repeat this exercise every time you catch yourself undervaluing or underestimating yourself. Replace your criticisms with acknowledgements. Do this until it becomes a habit.

At the end of this exercise, you will have recognized your achievements and strengths. This will be the third step in strengthening your self-esteem and self-efficacy.

Tackle challenges and seek learning.

The third and final step in strengthening your self-esteem and self-efficacy is to face challenges and seek to learn. Challenges are the difficult or challenging situations you face in life. Learning is the process of acquiring new knowledge or skills from experience.

Facing challenges and seeking learning is important to strengthen your self-esteem and self-efficacy. Because when you face challenges and seek learning, you test yourself, you overcome, you develop. You put yourself to the test, because you face situations that require you to leave your comfort zone, your routine, your security. You overcome, because you manage to solve problems, overcome obstacles, reach your goals. You develop, because you acquire new knowledge, skills, attitudes.

Facing challenges and seeking to learn makes you feel capable, competent and effective. It makes you feel that you can do what you set out to do, that you have the necessary resources, that you are in control of the situation. It makes you feel that you are a person with high confidence in yourself and your abilities.

To face challenges and seek learning, you can do the following exercise:

Take a sheet of paper and a pen.

Divide the sheet into three equal parts.

In each part, write one of the following headings: Past Challenges, Present Challenges, Future Challenges.

In the Past Challenges section, write down all the difficult or challenging situations you have experienced in your life that you have managed to overcome. You can think of situations related to all areas of your life: personal, professional, family, social, spiritual, etc. For example: I have overcome an illness. I have changed jobs. I have broken a relationship.

In the Present Challenges section, write down all the difficult or challenging situations that you are experiencing now or that you are going to experience soon and that you want to overcome. You can think of situations related to all areas of your life: personal, professional, family, social, spiritual, etc. For example: I am writing a book. I am looking for a promotion. I am in therapy.

In the Future Challenges section, write down all the difficult or challenging situations that you would like to experience in the future or that you think you will experience and that you want to overcome. You can think of situations related to all areas of your life: personal, professional, family, social, spiritual, etc. For example: I would like to travel the world. I think I am going to have a son or a daughter. I want to learn a language.

When you have finished writing down all your difficult or challenging situations, review what you have written and choose one from each part. The one that has marked you the most, the one that worries you the most, or the one that excites you the most.

For each of the three situations chosen, write below what you have learned or what you want to learn from that situation. You can think of a piece of knowledge, a skill or an attitude that you have acquired or want to acquire from that situation. For example: I have overcome an illness. I have learned to take care of my health and to value life.

When you have finished writing down all your learnings, review what you have written and practice saying the learnings out loud or mentally to yourself:

Do it with conviction, with emotion, with strength.

Repeat this exercise every time you face a challenge or seek to learn. Recognize what you have learned or what you want to learn from each situation. Do this until it becomes a habit.

At the end of this exercise, you will have faced the challenges and sought to learn. This will be the fourth and final step in strengthening your self-esteem and self-efficacy.

In this chapter, we have seen how to develop confidence in yourself and your capabilities. We have seen that confidence in yourself and your capabilities is the belief you have in your worth, your competence and your ability to achieve what you set out to do. We have seen that confidence in yourself and your abilities is fundamental to overcome life's obstacles with optimism and resilience.

We have also seen how to strengthen our confidence in ourselves and our capabilities. We have seen how to identify our limiting beliefs and how to change our internal dialogue and self-image. We have seen how to recognize our achievements and strengths and how to face challenges and seek learning.

I hope you found this chapter useful and interesting. I hope it has helped you to develop your confidence in yourself and your abilities. I hope it has encouraged you to hurry up the bad step and the good step.

In the next chapter, we will see how to manage the stress, anxiety and fear that paralyze or block us. We will see how to change our physiological, emotional and cognitive response to stressful situations. We will see how to use relaxation, breathing and meditation techniques.

But before moving on to the next chapter, I invite you to do a brief reflection exercise. I invite you to answer these questions:

What have you learned in this chapter?

What did you like most about this chapter?

What will you apply from this chapter in your life?

Write your answers on a piece of paper or in a journal. Share them with someone if you want to. And above all, put them into practice.

Remember: to the bad step give haste, to the good step also.

See you in the next chapter.

Suggestion:

Identify your limiting beliefs. They are those negative ideas or thoughts that you have about yourself, about your capabilities or about the world. They are those phrases that begin with "I can't", "I am not", "I don't have", "I don't deserve", "I don't know", etc. Recognize how they affect you, slow you down or block you.

Question your limiting beliefs. Do not accept them as absolute or immutable truths. Look for evidence that contradicts them, other ways of interpreting reality, other possibilities of acting. Change your limiting beliefs for empowering beliefs.

Change your internal dialogue. It is the conversation you have with yourself. Replace negative phrases with positive phrases. Use positive, affirmative, powerful words. Say things that encourage you, motivate you, inspire you.

Change your self-image. It is the mental image you have of yourself. Replace the negative image with a positive image. Use images, symbols, colors, etc. that represent, define or distinguish you. Show yourself how you would like to see yourself, how you want to be.

Recognize your achievements. They are the results you have achieved thanks to your effort, your dedication, your talent. Value what you have done, what you have learned, what you have grown. Reward your efforts, your sacrifices, your successes.

Recognize your strengths. These are the qualities that characterize you, the skills you possess, the resources you have. Appreciate what you are, what you can, what you have. Enhance your qualities, your skills, your resources.

Face the challenges. These are the difficult or challenging situations that come your way in life. Don't avoid or shy away from them. Face them with determination and confidence. Look for creative and effective solutions.

Seeks learning. It is the process of acquiring new knowledge or skills from experience. Don't dwell on mistakes or failures. Learn from them and move on. Seek new opportunities and experiences to learn and grow.

Surround yourself with positive and supportive people. They are those people who share your dreams, your values, your goals. Those people who support you, encourage you, help you. Those people who give you feedback, advice, guidance.

Enjoy the process and the present. Don't obsess about the future or the end result. Enjoy the journey, the learning, the growth. Enjoy the here and now, the moment, the experience.

Conclusion:

These are ten tips to develop confidence in yourself and your abilities. I hope you liked them and that you put them into practice.

Remember: confidence in yourself and your abilities is fundamental to overcome life's obstacles with optimism and resilience.

Remember: to the bad step give haste, to the good step also.

3. How to manage stress, anxiety and fear.

Have you ever felt overwhelmed by pressure, demand or uncertainty? Have you ever felt nervous about anticipation, worry or insecurity? Have you ever felt paralyzed by danger, threat or risk?

If your answer is yes, don't be alarmed. It is normal. We have all felt stress, anxiety or fear at one time or another. We have all experienced these emotions that alert us, prepare us and protect us from difficult or challenging situations in life.

Stress, anxiety and fear are adaptive and functional emotions. They are emotions that help us adapt and function better in the face of environmental demands. They are emotions that help us overcome life's obstacles with optimism and resilience.

Stress is the physiological, emotional and cognitive response that is activated when we perceive a situation as challenging, demanding or threatening. Stress helps us to mobilize our resources, increase our performance and meet the challenge.

Anxiety is the physiological, emotional and cognitive response that is activated when we anticipate a situation as uncertain, dangerous or negative. Anxiety helps us to be alert, to prevent risks and to avoid danger.

Fear is the physiological, emotional and cognitive response that is activated when we face a situation as real, imminent or serious. Fear helps us to react, to defend and protect ourselves from harm.

But stress, anxiety and fear can also be maladaptive and dysfunctional emotions. They are emotions that harm us when they are excessive, prolonged or irrational. They are emotions that prevent us from adapting and functioning well in the face of environmental demands. They are emotions that prevent us from overcoming life's obstacles with optimism and resilience.

Stress, anxiety and fear are maladaptive and dysfunctional emotions when:

They are disproportionate to the situation that provokes them.

They are maintained beyond what is necessary or useful.

They are based on erroneous or distorted perceptions of reality.

They interfere with our physical, mental or emotional well-being.

They impair our ability to think, feel or act appropriately.

When stress, anxiety and fear are maladaptive and dysfunctional emotions, they can have negative consequences for our health and performance. Some of these consequences are:

Physiological alterations: tachycardia, hypertension, sweating, tremors, insomnia, fatigue, headaches, digestive problems, etc.

Emotional disturbances: irritability, sadness, anguish, guilt, shame, frustration, apathy, etc.

Cognitive alterations: difficulty to concentrate, to remember, to make decisions, to solve problems, etc.

Behavioral alterations: avoidance, flight, aggressiveness, impulsivity, addictions, social isolation, etc.

Therefore, it is important that we know how to manage stress, anxiety and fear when they are maladaptive and dysfunctional emotions. That we know how to reduce or eliminate them when they are detrimental to us. That we know how to use or take advantage of them when they benefit us.

But how can we manage stress, anxiety and fear? How can we reduce or eliminate them when they harm us? How can we use or harness them when they benefit us?

To do so, I propose three steps:

What is stress, anxiety and fear and how do they affect your health and performance?

How to identify the sources and symptoms of stress, anxiety and fear.

How to apply relaxation, breathing and meditation techniques.

Let's look at each of them in more detail.

- What is stress, anxiety and fear and how do they affect your health and performance?

The first step in managing stress, anxiety and fear is to understand what they are and how they affect us. We have already seen this step in the introduction to this chapter, so we will not repeat it here. We will only remind you of its importance.

Understanding what stress, anxiety and fear are and how they affect us is important to manage them. Because when we understand what they are and how they affect us, we can recognize, accept and regulate them. We can recognize them, because we know how to identify their causes and symptoms. We can accept them, because we know that they are normal and natural. We can regulate them, because we know that they depend on our perception and our response.

So remember: understand what stress, anxiety and fear are and how they affect you.

- How to identify the sources and symptoms of stress, anxiety and fear.

The second step in managing stress, anxiety and fear is to identify their sources and symptoms. Sources are the situations or factors that provoke or trigger stress, anxiety or fear. Symptoms are the manifestations or signs that indicate or reveal the stress, anxiety or fear.

Identifying the sources and symptoms of stress, anxiety and fear is important to manage them. Because when we identify the sources and symptoms of stress, anxiety or fear, we can prevent, control or modify them. We can prevent them, because we know how to anticipate the situations or factors that provoke or trigger them. We can control them, because we know how to manage our reactions or emotions to the situations or factors that provoke or trigger them. We can modify them, because we know how to change the situations or factors that provoke or trigger them.

To identify the sources and symptoms of stress, anxiety and fear, you can do the following exercise:

Take a sheet of paper and a pen.

Divide the sheet into four equal parts.

In each part, write one of the following headings: Stress, Anxiety, Fear, Well-being.

In the Stress part, write down all the situations or factors that provoke or trigger stress in you. You can think of situations or factors related to all areas of your life: personal, professional, family, social, etc. For example: Having a lot of work. Having a tight deadline. Having a conflict with a colleague.

In the Anxiety part, write down all the situations or factors that provoke or trigger anxiety. You can think of situations or factors related to all areas of your life: personal, professional, family, social, etc. For example: Having to speak in public. Having to face a new situation. Having to make an important decision.

In the Fear part, write down all the situations or factors that provoke or trigger fear in you. You can think of situations or factors related to all areas of your life: personal, professional, family, social, etc. For example: Having to travel by plane. Having to go to the doctor. Having to face a real threat.

In the Well-being part, write down all the situations or factors that provoke or trigger well-being. You can think of situations or factors related to all areas of your life: personal, professional, family, social, etc. For example: Doing physical exercise. Listening to relaxing music. Being with loved ones.

When you have finished writing down all your situations or factors, review what you have written and choose one from each part. The one that most stresses you, distresses you, scares you, or relaxes you.

For each of the four situations or factors chosen, write below the symptoms you experience when you are in that situation or facing that factor. You can think of physiological, emotional, cognitive or behavioral symptoms that indicate or reveal your stress, anxiety, fear or well-being. For example: Being overworked. Symptoms: Tachycardia, irritability, difficulty concentrating, procrastination.

When you have finished writing down all your symptoms, review what you have written and practice identifying them when they arise in your daily life. Do it with attention, with objectivity, with acceptance.

Repeat this exercise every time you want to identify the sources and symptoms of stress, anxiety and fear. Do it until it becomes a habit.

At the end of this exercise, you will have identified the sources and symptoms of stress, anxiety and fear. This will be the second step in managing them.

- How to apply relaxation, breathing and meditation techniques.

The third and final step to manage stress, anxiety and fear is to apply relaxation, breathing and meditation techniques. These techniques are tools that help us reduce or eliminate stress, anxiety and fear when they are maladaptive and dysfunctional emotions. These techniques also help us to use or harness stress, anxiety and fear when they are adaptive and functional emotions.

Relaxation techniques are those that help us to relax our body and mind. They help us to release muscle tension, to lower the heart and respiratory rate, to calm the nervous system. They help us feel calmer, more comfortable, more rested.

Breathing techniques are those that help us to breathe in a conscious and controlled way. They help us to regulate the flow of oxygen and carbon dioxide in our body, to balance the blood pH, to stimulate the parasympathetic system. They help us to feel more alert, more energetic, more balanced.

Meditation techniques are those that help us to meditate in a conscious and focused way. They help us to focus our attention on an external or internal object (a sound, an image, a word), to observe our thoughts and emotions without judging or reacting to them, to cultivate our mindfulness. They help us to feel clearer, more serene, wiser.

Applying relaxation, breathing and meditation techniques is important to manage stress, anxiety and fear. Because when we apply these techniques, we can reduce or eliminate stress, anxiety and fear when they are maladaptive and dysfunctional emotions. We can use or harness stress, anxiety and fear when they are adaptive and functional emotions.

To apply relaxation, breathing and meditation techniques, you can do the following exercise:

Choose a quiet, comfortable place where you can be without interruptions or distractions.

Choose a relaxed, upright posture where you can stand without tension or discomfort.

Choose a time of the day when you can dedicate at least 10 minutes to this exercise.

Choose a relaxation, breathing or meditation technique that you like or want to try. You can look for information about the different techniques in books, magazines, internet, etc. or you can follow the instructions of a professional or an app.

Follow the steps of the chosen technique carefully, calmly, patiently. Don't worry if you don't do it perfectly or if you get distracted. Just go back to the technique and keep practicing.

When you finish the exercise, become aware of how you feel physically, emotionally and mentally. Compare how you feel before and after the exercise. Recognize the benefits of the technique.

Repeat this exercise every time you want to apply a relaxation, breathing or meditation technique. Do it until it becomes a habit.

At the end of this exercise, you will have applied a relaxation, breathing or meditation technique. This will be the third and final step in managing stress, anxiety and fear.

In this chapter, we have seen how to manage stress, anxiety and fear. We have seen that stress, anxiety and fear are adaptive and functional emotions that help us adapt and function better in the face of environmental demands. We have seen that stress, anxiety and fear can also be maladaptive and dysfunctional emotions that harm us when they are excessive, prolonged or irrational.

We have also seen how to manage stress, anxiety and fear when they are maladaptive and dysfunctional emotions. We have seen how to understand what they are and how they affect us. We have seen how to identify their sources and symptoms. We have seen how to apply relaxation, breathing and meditation techniques.

I hope you found this chapter useful and interesting. I hope it has helped you manage your stress, anxiety and fear. I hope it has encouraged you to hurry up the bad step and the good step.

In the next chapter, we will see how to cultivate optimism, hope and gratitude. We will see how to change the way we think, feel and act in a positive way. We will see how to use cognitive restructuring techniques, positive affirmations and gratitude journaling.

But before moving on to the next chapter, I invite you to do a brief reflection exercise. I invite you to answer these questions:

What have you learned in this chapter?

What did you like most about this chapter?

What will you apply from this chapter in your life?

Write your answers on a piece of paper or in a journal. Share them with someone if you want to. And above all, put them into practice.

Remember: to the bad step give haste, to the good step also.

See you in the next chapter.

Suggestion:

Understand what stress, anxiety and fear are and how they affect you. Do not see them as enemies but as allies that alert you, prepare you and protect you from difficult or challenging situations in life.

Recognize that these are normal and natural emotions that depend on your perception and response.

Identify the situations or factors that provoke or trigger stress, anxiety or fear. Do not avoid or deny them, but face them with determination and confidence. Look for creative and effective solutions to solve problems, overcome obstacles or achieve goals.

Identify the symptoms you experience when you feel stress, anxiety or fear. Do not ignore or repress them, but accept them with attention, objectivity and acceptance. Look for ways to alleviate or eliminate them to recover your physical, mental and emotional well-being.

Apply relaxation techniques to relax your body and mind. You can use techniques such as Jacobson's progressive, autogenic relaxation, autogenic training, etc. Practice these techniques regularly, calmly, patiently.

Apply breathing techniques to breathe in a conscious and controlled way. You can use techniques such as abdominal breathing, diaphragmatic breathing, alternate breathing, etc. Practice these techniques frequently, with energy, with balance.

Apply meditation techniques to meditate in a conscious and focused way. You can use techniques such as guided meditation, transcendental meditation, mindfulness meditation, etc. Practice these techniques with consistency, with clarity, with wisdom.

Surround yourself with positive and supportive people who will help you manage stress, anxiety and fear. Find people who share your dreams, your values, your goals. Look for people who support you, encourage you, help you. Look for people who will give you feedback, advice, guidance.

Take care of your physical and mental health by exercising, eating a balanced diet, getting enough sleep, avoiding toxic substances, etc. These habits will help you prevent or reduce stress, anxiety and fear. They will also help you to improve your mood, energy and self-esteem.

Enjoy your hobbies and leisure time by doing activities that you enjoy, that relax you, that amuse you. These activities will help you release stress, anxiety and fear. They will also help you to improve your creativity, motivation and satisfaction.

Accept what you cannot change and change what you cannot accept. Don't waste time and energy fighting the inevitable or the uncontrollable. Focus your attention and action on what you can do or improve. Be flexible, adaptable and resilient.

Conclusion:

These are ten tips for managing stress, anxiety and fear. I hope you liked them and that you put them into practice.

Remember: stress, anxiety and fear are adaptive and functional emotions that help you adapt and function better in the face of environmental demands.

Remember: to the bad step give haste, to the good step also.

4. How to cultivate gratitude, joy and humor.

Have you ever felt grateful for what you have, for what you are, for what you live? Have you ever felt joyful for what you do, for what you feel, for what you share? Have you ever felt funny for what you say, for what you hear, for what you laugh?

If your answer is yes, congratulations. That's great. We've all felt gratitude, joy and humor at one time or another. We've all experienced these positive emotions that fill us up, enlighten us and uplift us. We've all experienced these positive emotions that help us overcome life's obstacles with optimism and resilience.

Gratitude is the positive emotion that is activated when we recognize and value the good we have in our lives. Gratitude helps us appreciate who we are, what we have and what we live. Gratitude helps us feel happier, fuller and more fulfilled.

Joy is the positive emotion that is activated when we enjoy what we do, feel or share in our life. Joy helps us to enjoy what we like, what excites us or what we are passionate about. Joy helps us feel more alive, more energetic and more excited.

Humor is the positive emotion that is activated when we are amused by what we say, hear or laugh at in our lives. Humor helps us laugh at what surprises, shocks or amuses us. Humor helps us feel lighter, more creative and smarter.

Gratitude, joy and humor are positive emotions that are fundamental to our well-being and happiness. They are positive emotions that help us improve our physical, mental and emotional health. They are positive emotions that help us improve our social, family and professional relationships.

Gratitude, joy and humor are positive emotions that are fundamental to our well-being and happiness because:

They improve our physical health: reduce stress, anxiety and fear; strengthen the immune system; prevent disease; extend life.

They improve our mental health: increase optimism, hope and resilience; boost self-esteem and self-efficacy; promote learning; stimulate memory.

They improve our emotional health: generate pleasure, satisfaction and fulfillment; regulate negative emotions; foster balance; promote inner peace.

They improve our social relationships: they facilitate communication, empathy and understanding; they strengthen emotional bonds; they create a climate of trust; they spread good humor.

Therefore, it is important that we know how to cultivate gratitude, joy and humor in our lives. That we know how to express, feel and share them. That we know how to use them or take advantage of them to overcome life's obstacles with optimism and resilience.

But how can we cultivate gratitude, joy and humor? How can we express, feel and share them? How can we use or harness them to overcome life's obstacles with optimism and resilience?

To do so, I propose three steps:

What is gratitude, joy and humor and how do they benefit your well-being and happiness?

How to practice gratitude, joy and humor in your daily life.

How to spread gratitude, joy and humor to others.

Let's look at each of them in more detail.

- What is gratitude, joy and humor and how do they benefit your well-being and happiness?

The first step in cultivating gratitude, joy and humor is to understand what they are and how they benefit us. We have already seen this step in the introduction to this chapter, so we will not repeat it here. We will only remind you of its importance.

Understanding what gratitude, joy and humor are and how they benefit us is important to cultivate them. Because when we understand what they are and how they benefit us, we can recognize, value and enjoy them. We can recognize them, because we know how to identify their causes and their effects. We can value them, because we know they are essential and valuable. We can enjoy them, because we know that they depend on our attitude and our action.

So remember: understand what gratitude, joy and humor are and how they benefit you.

- How to practice gratitude, joy and humor in your daily life.

The second step to cultivating gratitude, joy and humor is to practice them in your day-to-day life. Practicing gratitude, joy and humor means expressing them, feeling them and sharing them consciously and frequently. It means making them a habit, a way of life, a philosophy.

Practicing gratitude, joy and humor in your day-to-day life is important to cultivate them. Because when you practice gratitude, joy and humor in your day-to-day life, you can reduce or eliminate the negative emotions that harm you. You can use or take advantage of the positive emotions that benefit you.

To practice gratitude, joy and humor in your daily life, you can do the following exercise:

Take a sheet of paper and a pen.

Divide the sheet into three equal parts.

In each part, write one of the following titles: Gratitude, Joy, Humor.

In the Gratitude part, write down three things you are grateful for today. They can be big or small, general or specific, material or immaterial. For example: I am grateful for my health, for my family, for my job.

In the Joy part, write down three things that have made you feel joyful today. They can be things you have done, things you have felt, or things you have shared. For example: It made me feel joyful to exercise, listen to my favorite song, talk to a friend.

Under Humor, write down three things that made you laugh today. They can be things you said, things you heard or things you saw. For example: I laughed at a joke I told, an anecdote I heard, a video I watched.

When you have finished writing all your things down, review what you have written and practice expressing them out loud or mentally. Do it with conviction, with emotion, with strength.

Repeat this exercise every day, preferably in the morning or evening. Do it until it becomes a habit.

At the end of this exercise, you will have practiced gratitude, joy and humor in your daily life. This will be the second step in cultivating them.

- How to spread gratitude, joy and humor to others.

The third and final step in cultivating gratitude, joy and humor is to spread them to others. Conveying gratitude, joy and humor means expressing them, feeling them and sharing them with the people around you. It means making them a gift, a form of communication, a philosophy.

Conveying gratitude, joy and humor to others is important to cultivate them. Because when you spread gratitude, joy and humor to others, you can improve your social, family and professional relationships. You can create a climate of trust, harmony and good humor.

To spread gratitude, joy and humor to others, you can do the following exercise:

Choose a person to whom you want to spread gratitude, joy and humor. It can be a person near or far, known or unknown, loved or indifferent.

Choose a way to communicate with that person. It can be a phone call, a text message, an email, a letter, a personal visit, etc.

Choose a way to express your gratitude, joy and humor. It can be a phrase, a word, a gesture, a symbol, etc. For example: Thank you for your support. It's good to see you. I'll tell you a joke.

Communicate with that person and express your gratitude, joy and humor with sincerity, enthusiasm and grace.

Observe how that person reacts to your communication. See if they feel grateful, joyful or amused. See if they return your gratitude, joy or humor.

Repeat this exercise every time you want to spread gratitude, joy and humor to someone. Do it until it becomes a habit.

At the end of this exercise, you will have passed on gratitude, joy and humor to someone. This will be the third and final step in cultivating them.

In this chapter, we have seen how to cultivate gratitude, joy and humor. We have seen that gratitude, joy and humor are positive emotions that are fundamental to our well-being and happiness. We have seen that gratitude, joy and humor help us improve our physical, mental and emotional health. We have seen that gratitude, joy and humor help us to improve our social, family and professional relationships.

We have also seen how to cultivate gratitude, joy and humor in our lives. We have seen how to understand what they are and how they benefit us. We have seen how to practice them in our daily lives. We have seen how to pass them on to others.

I hope you found this chapter useful and interesting. I hope it has helped you cultivate your gratitude, joy and humor. I hope it has encouraged you to hurry up the bad step and the good step.

In the next chapter we will see how to develop our personal strengths: those qualities or skills that make us unique and unrepeatable; those qualities or skills that make us shine.

But before moving on to the next chapter, I invite you to do a brief reflection exercise. I invite you to answer these questions:

What have you learned in this chapter?

What did you like most about this chapter?

What will you apply from this chapter in your life?

Write your answers on a piece of paper or in a journal. Share them with someone if you want to. And above all, put them into practice.

Remember: to the bad step give haste, to the good step also.

See you in the next chapter.

Suggestion:

Understand what gratitude, joy and humor are and how they benefit you. Don't see them as luxuries but as needs that fill you, enlighten you and uplift you. Recognize that these are positive emotions that depend on your attitude and action.

Practice gratitude every day by recognizing and appreciating the good you have in your life. Take nothing for granted or for granted. Be grateful for what you are, what you have and what you live. Be grateful for people, things, circumstances.

Practice joy every day by enjoying what you do, feel or share in your life. Don't lose yourself in the past or the future. Enjoy the present, the moment, the experience. Enjoy what you like, what excites you or what you are passionate about.

Practice humor every day by having fun with what you say, hear or laugh at in your life. Don't take everything so seriously or so personally. Laugh at what surprises, shocks or amuses you. Laugh at yourself, at others, at life.

Convey gratitude to others by expressing your appreciation and appreciation for what they do, feel or are. Don't wait until it's late or until it's necessary. Tell them thank you for their support, their affection, their presence. Tell them thank you with words, with gestures, with actions.

Spread the joy to others by sharing with them your moments of pleasure, satisfaction and fulfillment. Don't keep them just for yourself or for special occasions. Invite them to do something that you like, that excites you or that you are passionate about. Invite them with enthusiasm, with energy, with illusion.

Spread humor to others by making them laugh with your witticisms, your anecdotes or your jokes. Don't bore them with your problems, complaints or criticisms. Tell them something that surprises, shocks or amuses them. Tell them with grace, with wit, with irony.

Take care of your physical and mental health by exercising, eating a balanced diet, getting enough sleep, avoiding toxic substances, etc. These habits will help you prevent or reduce the negative emotions that harm you. They will also help you to improve your mood, energy and self-esteem.

Enjoy your hobbies and leisure time by doing activities that you enjoy, that relax you, that amuse you. These activities will help you release stress, anxiety and fear. They will also help you to improve your creativity, motivation and satisfaction.

Be optimistic, hopeful and resilient in the face of difficult or challenging life situations. Do not let yourself be overcome by pessimism, hopelessness or fragility. Look for the positive side, opportunities and solutions in every situation. Be flexible, adaptable and persevering.

Conclusion:

These are ten tips for cultivating gratitude, joy and humor. I hope you liked them and that you put them into practice.

Remember: gratitude, joy and humor are positive emotions that are fundamental to your well-being and happiness.

Remember: to the bad step give haste, to the good step also.

5. How to communicate effectively and create positive relationships.

Have you ever communicated with someone in a clear, precise and coherent way? Have you ever felt listened to, understood, valued and appreciated? Have you established a relationship of trust, respect and collaboration?

If your answer is yes, fantastic. That's wonderful. We've all communicated effectively with someone at one time or another. We've all established a positive relationship. We have all experienced the benefits of effective communication and positive relationships. We have all experienced the benefits of effective communication and positive relationships that help us overcome life's obstacles with optimism and resilience.

Effective communication is the process of exchanging information, ideas, feelings or emotions between two or more people in a clear, precise and coherent way. Effective communication helps us to express what we think, feel or want. Effective communication helps us understand what others think, feel or want.

Positive relationships are the affective, social or professional bond that is established between two or more people based on trust, respect and collaboration. Positive relationships help us feel supported, valued and loved. Positive relationships help us to support, value and love others.

Effective communication and positive relationships are critical to our personal and professional success. They are critical to our personal and professional success because:

They improve our self-esteem and self-efficacy: they make us feel more confident, more competent and more capable.

They improve our well-being and happiness: they make us feel more satisfied, fuller and more fulfilled.

They improve our physical, mental and emotional health: they make us feel healthier, more balanced and calmer.

They improve our social and interpersonal skills: they make us more empathetic, more assertive and more persuasive.

They improve our performance and productivity: they make us more creative, more innovative and more efficient.

Therefore, it is important that we know how to communicate effectively and create positive relationships in our lives. That we know how to express, listen and understand. That we know how to trust, respect and collaborate.

But how can we communicate effectively and build positive relationships? How can we express, listen and understand? How can we trust, respect and collaborate?

To do so, I propose three steps:

What is effective communication and why is it key to personal and professional success?

How to improve your active listening, assertiveness and feedback skills.

How to build relationships of trust, respect and collaboration.

Let's look at each of them in more detail.

- What is effective communication and why is it key to personal and professional success?

The first step to communicating effectively and building positive relationships is to understand what effective communication is and why it is key to personal and professional success. We have already covered this step in the introduction to this chapter, so we will not repeat it here. We will just remind you of its importance.

Understanding what effective communication is and why it is key to personal and professional success is important to communicating effectively and building positive relationships. Because when we understand what effective communication is and why it is key to personal and professional success, we can recognize it, value it and practice it. We can recognize it, because we know how to identify its elements, its types and its levels. We can value it, because we know that it is essential and beneficial. We can practice it, because we know that it depends on our attitude and our ability.

So remember: understand what effective communication is and why it is key to personal and professional success.

- How to improve your active listening, assertiveness and feedback skills.

The second step to communicate effectively and create positive relationships is to improve our active listening, assertiveness and feedback skills. These skills are what allow us to express, listen and understand effectively. These skills are what allow us to communicate clearly, accurately and consistently.

Improving our active listening, assertiveness and feedback skills is important to communicate effectively and create positive relationships. Because when we improve our active listening, assertiveness and feedback skills, we can express what we think, feel or want in a respectful, honest and constructive way. We can listen to what others think, feel or want in an attentive, empathetic and understanding way. We can understand what others tell us, show us or ask us in an objective, critical and collaborative way.

To improve our active listening, assertiveness and feedback skills, you can do the following exercise:

Choose a person with whom you want to communicate effectively and create a positive relationship. It can be a person near or far, known or unknown, loved or indifferent.

Choose a way to communicate with that person. It can be a phone call, a text message, an email, a letter, a personal visit, etc.

Choose a time of day when you can communicate with that person. It can be in the morning, afternoon or evening. It can be before or after an important or routine activity.

Choose a topic about which you want to communicate with that person. It can be personal or professional, general or specific, positive or negative.

Communicate with that person using the following skills:

Active listening: pay attention to what the person is saying without interrupting or being distracted. Show interest in what he/she is telling you with your verbal (words) and non-verbal (gestures) language. Ask open-ended questions to clarify or deepen what he/she is saying. Paraphrase or summarize what he/she says to verify that you have understood it well.

Assertiveness: express what you think, feel or want on the subject without attacking or submitting to that person. Use first person sentences (I) to express your point of view without imposing or denying it. Use positive phrases (yes) to express your agreement or disagreement without offending or hurting that person. Use constructive phrases (and) to express your proposal or solution without criticizing or rejecting that person.

Feedback: gives or receives information about the topic in a respectful, honest and constructive way. Uses specific phrases (what) to give or receive information about specific facts without generalizing or exaggerating. Uses factual sentences (how) to give or receive information about observable behaviors without judging or interpreting. Uses collaborative sentences (what for) to give or receive information about common goals without imposing or giving in.

Observe how communication with that person develops using these skills. See if effective communication and a positive relationship occurs. Observe if an understanding, agreement or solution is reached.

Repeat this exercise every time you want to communicate effectively and create a positive relationship with someone. Do it until it becomes a habit.

At the end of this exercise, you will have improved your active listening, assertiveness and feedback skills. This will be the second step in communicating effectively and creating positive relationships.

- How to build relationships of trust, respect and collaboration.

The third and final step in communicating effectively and creating positive relationships is to build relationships of trust, respect and collaboration. These relationships are the ones that allow us to communicate clearly, accurately and consistently. These relationships are the ones that allow us to create an emotional, social or professional bond based on trust, respect and collaboration.

Building relationships of trust, respect and collaboration is important for communicating effectively and creating positive relationships. Because when we build relationships of trust, respect and collaboration, we can feel supported, valued and loved by others. We can support, value and love others.

To build relationships of trust, respect and collaboration, you can do the following exercise:

Choose a person with whom you want to build a relationship of trust, respect and collaboration. It can be a person near or far, known or unknown, loved or indifferent.

Choose a way to relate to that person. It can be a phone call, a text message, an email, a letter, a personal visit, etc.

Choose a time of day when you can relate to that person. It can be in the morning, afternoon or evening. It can be before or after an important or routine activity.

Relate to that person using the following principles:

Confidence: show that person that you trust him or her and that you can be reliable. Be honest with her about what you think, feel or want. Keep your commitments to her about what you say, do or promise. Acknowledge your mistakes with her and apologize if necessary.

Respect: show the person that you respect him/her and that you expect to be respected. Accept their differences without discriminating or belittling them. Value her opinions with her without imposing or denying her yours. Recognize her rights with her and respect her limits if she has them.

Collaboration: show the person that you want to collaborate with him/her and that you expect his/her collaboration. Look for common ground with them without giving up or imposing your interests. Negotiate solutions with her without giving in or gaining everything you want. Work as a team with her without competing or depending on what she does.

Observe how the relationship with that person develops using these principles. Observe if a relationship of trust, respect and collaboration is produced. Observe if an affective, social or professional bond is achieved.

Repeat this exercise every time you want to build a relationship of trust, respect and collaboration with someone. Do it until it becomes a habit.

At the end of this exercise, you will have built a relationship of trust, respect and collaboration with someone. This will be the third and final step in communicating effectively and building positive relationships.

In this chapter we have seen how to communicate effectively and create positive relationships. We have seen that effective communication is the process of exchanging information, ideas, feelings or emotions between two or more people in a clear, precise and coherent manner. We have seen that positive relationships are the emotional, social or professional bond that is established between two or more people based on trust, respect and collaboration.

We have also seen how to communicate effectively and create positive relationships in our lives. We have seen how to understand what effective communication is and why it is key to personal and professional success. We have seen how to improve our active listening, assertiveness and feedback skills. We have seen how to build relationships of trust, respect and collaboration.

I hope you found this chapter useful and interesting. I hope it has helped you communicate effectively and build positive relationships. I hope that it has encouraged you to make haste to the wrong step and the right step.

In the next chapter we will see how to develop our personal potential: that which makes us unique and unrepeatable; that which makes us shine.

But before moving on to the next chapter, I invite you to do a brief reflection exercise. I invite you to answer these questions:

What have you learned in this chapter?

What did you like most about this chapter?

What will you apply from this chapter in your life?

Write your answers on a piece of paper or in a journal. Share them with someone if you want. And above all, put them into practice.

Remember: to the bad step give haste, to the good step also.

See you in the next chapter.

Suggestion:

Understand what effective communication is and why it is key to personal and professional success. Do not see it as an innate ability but as a skill that can be learned and improved. Recognize that it is a complex and dynamic process that depends on several factors.

Improve your active listening skills by paying attention to what others tell you without interrupting or distracting them. Show interest in what they are saying with your verbal and nonverbal language. Ask open-ended questions to clarify or elaborate on what they are saying. Paraphrase or summarize what they say to verify that you have understood it well.

Improve your assertiveness skills by expressing what you think, feel or want without attacking or submitting to others. Use first person sentences to express your point of view without imposing or denying it. Use positive phrases to express your agreement or disagreement without offending or hurting others. Use constructive phrases to express your proposal or solution without criticizing or rejecting others.

Improve your feedback skills by giving or receiving information about the topic in a respectful, honest and constructive manner. Use specific phrases to give or receive information about specific facts without generalizing or exaggerating. Uses objective sentences to give or receive information about observable behaviors without judging or interpreting. Uses collaborative phrases to give or receive information about common goals without imposing or giving in.

Build trusting relationships by showing others that you trust them and can be trusted. Be honest with others about what you think, feel or want. Keep your commitments to others about what you say, do or promise. Acknowledge your mistakes with others and apologize if necessary.

Build respectful relationships by showing others that you respect them and expect to be respected. Accept differences with others without discriminating against or belittling them. Values the opinions of others without imposing or denying them yours. Recognize the rights of others and respect their limits if they have them.

Build collaborative relationships by showing others that you want to collaborate with them and expect their cooperation. Seek common ground with others without giving up or imposing your interests. Negotiate solutions with others without giving in or gaining everything you want. Work as a team with others without competing or depending on what they do.

Take care of your non-verbal communication, i.e., the set of gestures, expressions, postures, voice tones, etc., that accompany your verbal communication, i.e., the words you use. Make sure that your non-verbal communication is consistent with your verbal communication, i.e., that it conveys the same message and the same intention.

Adapt your communication to the context, that is, to the set of circumstances surrounding the communicative situation, such as place, time, motive, objective, etc. Make sure that your communication is appropriate to the context, i.e. that it respects the norms, expectations and needs of the communicative situation.

Enrich your communication by using resources such as humor, creativity, empathy, etc., that help you capture attention, generate interest and create a connection with others. Make sure these resources are appropriate to the topic, tone and purpose of your communication.

Conclusion:

These are ten tips for communicating effectively and building positive relationships. I hope you liked them and that you put them into practice.

Remember: effective communication and positive relationships are critical to your personal and professional success.

Remember: to the bad step give haste, to the good step also.

6. How to learn from mistakes and failures.

Have you ever made a mistake or failed at some point in your life? Have you felt shame, guilt or fear because of it? Have you learned anything or improved anything because of it?

If your answer is yes, don't worry. It's normal. We've all made mistakes and failed at some point in our lives. We have all felt shame, guilt or fear because of it. We have all learned something or improved something because of it.

Mistakes and failures are part of life. They are part of the learning and improvement process. They are part of the process of personal and professional growth. They are part of the process of overcoming life's obstacles with optimism and resilience.

An error is an action or decision that does not produce the expected or desired result. An error can be involuntary or voluntary, conscious or unconscious, simple or complex, slight or serious, etc. An error can have positive or negative consequences, for oneself or for others.

A failure is a result or a state that does not meet expectations or previous objectives. A failure can be temporary or permanent, partial or total, individual or collective, etc. A failure can have positive or negative consequences, for oneself or for others.

Mistakes and failures are inevitable and indispensable for growth. They are inevitable because no one is perfect or infallible. We are all human and we all make mistakes and fail. They are indispensable because they help us learn and improve. They help us grow.

Mistakes and failures help us learn and improve because:

They show us what does not work, what we do not know, what we cannot.

They motivate us to seek solutions, to acquire knowledge, to develop skills.

They challenge us to surpass ourselves, to innovate, to create.

They teach us values such as humility, responsibility and perseverance.

They make us stronger, wiser, more resilient.

Therefore, it is important that we learn from the mistakes and failures in our lives. That we know how to recognize them, accept them and take advantage of them. That we know how to transform them into opportunities and lessons.

But how can we learn from mistakes and failures? How can we recognize, accept and take advantage of them? How can we transform them into opportunities and lessons?

To do so, I propose three steps:

What are mistakes and failures and why are they inevitable and indispensable for growth?

How to adopt a learning and continuous improvement mentality.

How to transform mistakes and failures into opportunities and lessons.

Let's look at each of them in more detail.

- What are mistakes and failures and why are they inevitable and indispensable for growth?

The first step in learning from mistakes and failures is to understand what they are and why they are inevitable and indispensable for growth. We have already seen this step in the introduction to this chapter, so we will not repeat it here. We will only remind you of its importance.

Understanding what mistakes and failures are and why they are inevitable and indispensable for growth is important for learning from them. Because when we understand what mistakes and failures are and why they are inevitable and indispensable for growth, we can change our attitude towards them. We can stop seeing them as threats or punishments and start seeing them as challenges or opportunities. We can stop feeling shame, guilt or fear about them and start feeling curious, interested or excited about them. We can stop avoiding, denying or hiding them and start facing, recognizing and taking advantage of them.

So remember: understand what mistakes and failures are and why they are inevitable and indispensable for growth.

- How to adopt a learning and continuous improvement mentality.

The second step in learning from mistakes and failures is to adopt a learning and continuous improvement mindset. A learning and continuous improvement mindset is one that allows us to see mistakes and failures as sources of information, feedback and progress. A learning and continuous improvement mindset is one that allows us to see success as a process, not a destination.

Adopting a learning and continuous improvement mindset is important to learn from mistakes and failures. Because when we adopt a mindset of learning and continuous improvement, we can change the way we think, feel and act in the face of mistakes and failures. We can think of them as normal and natural, as part of the journey, as opportunities to learn and improve. We can feel that they are challenges and motivations, that they are stimuli to improve ourselves, that they are lessons to grow. We can act with responsibility and proactivity, with humility and perseverance, with creativity and innovation.

To adopt a learning and continuous improvement mindset, you can do the following exercise:

Take a sheet of paper and a pen.

Divide the sheet into two equal parts.

In each part, write one of the following titles: Fixed Mindset, Growth Mindset.

In the Fixed Mindset part, write down the beliefs, feelings and behaviors that characterize a person who has a fixed mindset in the face of mistakes and failures. For example: I believe that success depends on talent or luck. I feel shame, guilt or fear when I make a mistake or failure. I avoid difficult or challenging situations so as not to make a mistake or fail.

In the Growth Mindset part, write the beliefs, feelings, and behaviors that characterize a person who has a growth mindset in the face of mistakes and failures. For example: I believe that success depends on effort or perseverance. I am curious, interested or excited when I make a mistake or fail. I face difficult or challenging situations to learn or improve.

When you have finished writing both parts, review what you have written and compare the differences between a fixed mindset and a growth mindset. Reflect on what mindset you have about mistakes and failures. Reflect on what mindset you want to have about mistakes and failures.

Analyze how you thought, felt and acted in that situation using the Fixed Mindset part. Write down what you thought, felt and acted on a piece of paper.

Analyze how you might have thought, felt and acted in that situation using the Growth Mindset part. Write down what you might have thought, felt and acted on another piece of paper.

Compare what you wrote on both papers and note the differences between a fixed mindset and a growth mindset. Notice how your view of error or failure changes according to your mindset. See how your view of failure or failure changes depending on your mindset. See how your mindset changes the way you feel and act in the face of error or failure. See how your way of learning and improving from error or failure changes according to your mindset.

Repeat this exercise every time you make a mistake or fail at something. Do this until you adopt a mindset of learning and continuous improvement.

At the end of this exercise, you will have adopted a mindset of learning and continuous improvement. This will be the second step in learning from mistakes and failures.

- How to transform mistakes and failures into opportunities and lessons.

The third and final step in learning from mistakes and failures is to transform them into opportunities and lessons. Transforming mistakes and failures into opportunities and lessons means seeing them as sources of information, feedback and progress. It means seeing them as challenges or opportunities to learn and improve. It means seeing them as experiences or lessons for growth.

Transforming mistakes and failures into opportunities and lessons is important to learn from them. Because when we transform mistakes and failures into opportunities and lessons, we can change the way we react to them. We can react with responsibility and proactivity, with humility and perseverance, with creativity and innovation.

To transform mistakes and failures into opportunities and lessons, you can do the following exercise:

Choose a recent situation in which you made a mistake or failed at something. It can be a personal or professional situation, big or small, important or trivial.

Analyze that situation using the following questions:

What happened? Describe what happened with concrete and objective facts.

What did you want? Describe what you expected or wanted to achieve with your actions or decisions.

What did I do? Describe what you did or decided to do about the situation.

What did I achieve? Describe what you did or did not accomplish by your actions or decisions.

What did I feel? Describe what you felt or did not feel with your actions or decisions.

What did I learn? Describe what you learned or did not learn from your actions or decisions.

What can I improve? Describe what you can improve or not improve with your actions or decisions.

Write the answers to these questions on a piece of paper or in a journal.

Review the answers you have written and look for the opportunities and lessons behind the mistake or failure. Look for the information, feedback and progress offered by the mistake or failure. Look for the learning, improvement and growth offered by the mistake or failure.

Write down the opportunities and lessons you have encountered on another piece of paper or in another journal.

Compare what you wrote in both papers or journals and see how you have transformed the mistake or failure into an opportunity and a lesson. Notice how you have changed the way you look at the mistake or failure. Notice how you have changed the way you feel and act in the face of the mistake or failure. See how you have changed the way you learn and improve from the mistake or failure.

Repeat this exercise every time you make a mistake or fail at something. Do it until you transform mistakes and failures into opportunities and lessons.

At the end of this exercise, you will have transformed mistakes and failures into opportunities and lessons. This will be the third and final step to learn from them.

In this chapter we have seen how to learn from mistakes and failures. We have seen that mistakes and failures are part of life, of the process of learning and improvement, of the process of personal and professional growth. We have seen that mistakes and failures are inevitable and indispensable for growth.

We have also seen how to learn from mistakes and failures in our lives. We have seen how to understand what they are and why they are inevitable and indispensable for growth. We have seen how to adopt a mindset of learning and continuous improvement. We have seen how to transform mistakes and failures into opportunities and lessons.

I hope you found this chapter useful and interesting. I hope it has helped you learn from your mistakes and failures. I hope it has encouraged you to hurry up the wrong step and the right step.

In the next chapter we will see how to develop our emotional intelligence: that capacity that allows us to recognize, understand and manage our emotions and those of others.

But before moving on to the next chapter, I invite you to do a brief reflection exercise. I invite you to answer these questions:

What have you learned in this chapter?

What did you like most about this chapter?

What will you apply from this chapter in your life?

Write your answers on a piece of paper or in a journal. Share them with someone if you want to. And above all, put them into practice.

Remember: to the bad step give haste, to the good step also.

See you in the next chapter.

Suggestion:

Understand what mistakes and failures are and why they are inevitable and indispensable for growth. Do not see them as failures but as results. Do not see them as endings but as beginnings. Do not see them as obstacles but as opportunities.

Adopt a learning and continuous improvement mentality. Don't settle for what you know or can do. Always seek to learn something new or improve something old. Do not compare yourself with others but with yourself. Always seek to surpass yourself.

Transform mistakes and failures into opportunities and lessons. Don't ignore or deny them. Analyze them and learn from them. Do not regret or suffer them. Accept them and take advantage of them. Do not repeat or avoid them. Correct them and prevent them.

Acknowledge your mistakes and failures with humility and responsibility. Do not hide or excuse them. Admit them and accept them. Do not attribute them to external or outside factors. Acknowledge your share of blame or influence. Do not blame or punish yourself for them. Forgive yourself and others.

Learn from your mistakes and failures with curiosity and interest. Don't stay on the surface or the result. Investigate the causes and consequences. Don't dwell on the past or the problem. Look for solutions and alternatives. Don't stay in the theory or on paper. Apply what you learn in practice or action.

Improve your mistakes and failures with effort and perseverance. Don't give up or get discouraged by them. Try again or try something else. Don't settle or get stuck with them. Seek to improve or look for another path. Don't limit yourself or shut yourself off because of them. Broaden your horizons or your possibilities.

Share your mistakes and failures with honesty and generosity. Don't keep them only to yourself or for your privacy. Communicate them to others or ask for help if you need it. Don't use them to brag or to victimize yourself. Use them to teach or to learn from others.

Celebrate your mistakes and failures with humor and optimism. Don't give them more importance than they have or deserve. Laugh at them or make jokes about them. Don't give them a negative or fatalistic meaning. Give them a positive or hopeful meaning.

Appreciate your mistakes and failures with gratitude and recognition. Don't see them as punishments or misfortunes. See them as gifts or blessings. Don't see them as losses or defeats. See them as gains or victories.

Be inspired by your mistakes and failures with creativity and innovation. Don't see them as barriers or limitations. See them as challenges or inspirations. Don't see them as endings or closings. See them as beginnings or openings.

Conclusion:

These are ten tips to learn from your mistakes and failures. I hope you liked them and that you put them into practice.

Remember: mistakes and failures are part of life, of the learning and improvement process, of the personal and professional growth process.

Remember: to the bad step give haste, to the good step also.

7. How to adapt to change and uncertainty.

Change and uncertainty are two realities that characterize today's world. We live in a time of constant transformations, technological advances, economic crises, social conflicts and environmental challenges. All this generates a volatile, complex and ambiguous environment that tests our ability to adapt.

Change and uncertainty can affect our stability and security. We may feel disoriented, confused, threatened. We may experience stress, anxiety, fear. We may resist change, cling to the past, deny reality.

But we can also see change and uncertainty as an opportunity, as a stimulus, as a challenge. We can embrace change, adapt to the present, create the future. We can experience curiosity, enthusiasm, confidence. We can embrace change, innovate, grow.

To do so, we need to develop three key skills: flexibility, resilience and tolerance of ambiguity. These skills enable us to adjust to new circumstances, overcome difficulties and manage uncertainty effectively.

- What is change and uncertainty and how do they affect your stability and security?

Change is the modification or alteration of something. Change can be positive or negative, expected or unexpected, gradual or sudden. Change can affect different areas of our lives: personal, family, work, social, etc.

Uncertainty is the lack of certainty or knowledge about something. Uncertainty can be objective or subjective, temporary or permanent, slight or severe. Uncertainty can be related to different aspects of our reality: the past, the present or the future.

Change and uncertainty affect our stability and security because they force us to leave our comfort zone, our usual or preferred state.

They confront us with new, unknown or unpredictable situations that can generate doubts, risks or threats.

For example:

A change of job can affect our economic and professional stability.

A sentimental breakup can affect our emotional and affective stability.

A pandemic can affect our health and social security.

These situations can cause us stress, anxiety or fear because they make us feel vulnerable, insecure or powerless. These emotions can interfere with our well-being and performance.

- How to develop flexibility, resilience and tolerance for ambiguity.

Flexibility is the ability to adapt to different situations or conditions that arise. Flexibility implies being able to modify our behavior, our attitudes or our beliefs as circumstances require.

Resilience is the ability to overcome adversity or trauma. Resilience implies being able to recover from pain, suffering or failure and emerge stronger from them.

Tolerance of ambiguity is the ability to handle uncertainty without becoming distressed or paralyzed. Tolerance of ambiguity involves being able to accept a lack of clarity, control or predictability and act with confidence and decisiveness.

These three skills are fundamental to adapt to change and uncertainty successfully. They help us face challenges with optimism and resilience. They allow us to see the positive side of things and find the opportunities in every situation.

To develop these skills we can follow these tips:

Be aware of our thoughts and emotions in the face of change and uncertainty. Identify those that are negative or irrational and replace them with more positive or rational ones.

Be flexible with ourselves and with others. Accept that we are not perfect, that we can make mistakes, that we can change. Accept that others also have their own opinions, needs and preferences.

To be resilient in the face of difficulties. Learn from mistakes, failures and losses. Seek the support of people who love and value us. Take care of our physical and mental health.

Be tolerant of ambiguity. Do not seek absolute certainties, but reasonable probabilities. Do not pretend to control everything, but assume calculated risks. Do not anticipate the worst, but hope for the best.

- How to anticipate change and take advantage of innovation.

Change and uncertainty are not only inevitable, but also necessary. Change and uncertainty are drivers of progress, development and evolution. Change and uncertainty offer us the possibility to improve, to innovate, to create.

To take advantage of change and uncertainty we can follow these steps:

Anticipate change. Be attentive to environmental signals, market trends, and society's demands. Be informed, updated and prepared for change.

Take advantage of innovation. Be open to new ideas, new methods, new products. Be willing to experiment, to test, to learn. Be motivated by the desire to excel, to differentiate, to add value.

Leading change. Be willing to assume the role of agents of change, promoters of innovation, creators of solutions. Be able to communicate, persuade and mobilize others towards change.

In this chapter we have seen how we can adapt to change and uncertainty with optimism and resilience. We have learned what change and uncertainty are and how they affect our stability and security. We have discovered how to develop flexibility, resilience and tolerance for ambiguity. And we have explored how to anticipate change and take advantage of innovation.

Hurrying to the wrong step implies accepting change and uncertainty as part of life. It involves adapting to the present with flexibility, overcoming adversity with resilience and managing uncertainty with tolerance. It involves anticipating the future with curiosity, seizing opportunities with enthusiasm and leading progress with confidence.

If you apply what you have learned in this chapter, you will see how you feel more capable, more confident, more satisfied. You will see how you become more adaptable, more resilient, more innovative.

Suggestion:

Accept change and uncertainty as part of life. Do not see them as threats, but as opportunities. Do not resist change, but flow with it. Don't be distressed by uncertainty, but embrace it.

Be aware of your thoughts and emotions in the face of change and uncertainty. Identify those that are negative or irrational and replace them with more positive or rational ones. For example, instead of thinking "I can't do this", think "I can learn to do this".

Be flexible with your plans, your expectations and your objectives. Adapt your actions to new circumstances or conditions that arise. Do not stick to what no longer works or is no longer useful. Look for alternatives, solutions or improvements.

Be resilient in the face of difficulties, failures or losses you may suffer due to change or uncertainty. Don't be overcome by pain, suffering or frustration. Learn from experience, draw lessons and strengths. Regain your balance and energy.

Be tolerant of ambiguity, lack of clarity or lack of control you may feel because of change or uncertainty. Do not seek absolute certainties, but reasonable probabilities. Don't pretend to control everything, but take calculated risks. Do not anticipate the worst, but expect the best.

Stay informed, updated and prepared for change and uncertainty. Study the trends, developments, demands and opportunities in your environment. Acquire the knowledge, skills and competencies you need to adapt to change and uncertainty.

He takes advantage of innovation, new ideas, new methods, new products that arise from change and uncertainty. Is open to experiment, to try, to learn new things. Is motivated by the desire to excel, to differentiate yourself, to add value.

Lead change and innovation in your personal or professional environment. Be an agent of change, a promoter of innovation, a creator of solutions. Communicate your vision, persuade others and mobilize your team towards change and innovation.

Seek the support of people who love you and value you in the face of change and uncertainty. Share your doubts, your fears, your concerns with them. Ask for their advice, their help, their opinion. Thank them for their presence, their trust, their collaboration.

Take care of your physical and mental health in the face of change and uncertainty. Practice healthy habits such as a balanced diet, adequate rest and regular physical activity. Engage in activities that relax, entertain and satisfy you, such as reading, listening to music or meditating.

Conclusion

These are ten detailed tips for adapting to change and uncertainty with optimism and resilience. If you follow them, you will see how you feel more capable, more confident, more satisfied in the face of change and uncertainty.

Remember that to take the wrong step in haste implies accepting change and uncertainty as part of life. It involves adapting to the present with flexibility, overcoming adversity with resilience and managing uncertainty with tolerance. It involves anticipating the future with curiosity, seizing opportunities with enthusiasm and leading progress with confidence.

I hope you liked these detailed tips for chapter 7. If you want me to help you with anything else, just ask me.

8. How to take advantage of your creativity and passion.

Creativity and passion are two qualities that make us feel alive, that make us enjoy what we do, that make us stand out. Creativity and passion are sources of motivation and satisfaction. Creativity and passion are essential ingredients to make the wrong step go faster.

Creativity is the ability to generate original, novel or useful ideas. Creativity involves using our imagination, intuition and divergent thinking. Creativity allows us to solve problems, create works or innovate products.

Passion is the feeling of love, enthusiasm or interest for something or someone. Passion implies having a vocation, a purpose or a dream. Passion allows us to dedicate ourselves to what we like, to what makes us happy, to what gives us meaning.

To tap into our creativity and passion we need to discover our talent, our calling and our purpose. We need to know what we are good at, what we are passionate about and what we want to contribute to the world. And we need to express our creativity and passion in our personal and professional projects.

- What is creativity and passion and how do they enhance your motivation and satisfaction?

Creativity and passion are two qualities that enhance our motivation and satisfaction. Motivation is the impulse or force that moves us to do something. Satisfaction is the pleasure or joy we feel when we do something.

Creativity boosts our motivation because it makes us feel curious, challenging, competent. It makes us look for new challenges, new solutions, new opportunities. It makes us feel proud of our ideas, our works, our innovations.

Passion boosts our motivation because it makes us feel engaged, excited, inspired. It makes us pursue our dreams, our goals, our ideals. It makes us feel happy to do what we like, what fulfills us, what gives us meaning.

Creativity enhances our satisfaction because it makes us feel fulfilled, valued, recognized. It makes us enjoy the creative process, the creative result, the creative impact. It makes us feel that we have contributed something unique, something new, something useful.

Passion enhances our satisfaction because it makes us feel full, connected, transcendent. It makes us enjoy the journey, the destiny, the legacy. It makes us feel that we have lived with love, with enthusiasm, with interest.

- How to discover your talent, your vocation and your purpose.

To discover your talent, your vocation and your purpose you can follow these steps:

Identify your natural or acquired skills. Think about what you are good at, what you excel at, what you find easy or fun to do.

Identify your personal or professional interests. Think about what you like to do, what you are passionate about, what excites you and what excites you.

Identify your personal or professional values. Think about what you care about doing, what you are committed to, what identifies or defines you.

Look for the intersection between your skills, your interests and your values. That intersection is your talent: what you are good at doing and like to do and care about doing.

Find a way to apply your talent to a specific area of your personal or professional life. That way is your vocation: what you can do with your talent to satisfy your own or someone else's need.

Look for the meaning of applying your vocation to that particular area of your personal or professional life. That meaning is your purpose:

what you want to achieve with your vocation to contribute to the greater good.

- How to express your creativity and passion in your personal and professional projects.

To express your creativity and passion in your personal and professional projects you can follow these tips:

Choose projects that are aligned with your talent, your vocation and your purpose. Projects that allow you to use your skills, your interests and your values. Projects that make you feel motivated, satisfied and fulfilled.

Plan your projects with clarity, realism and flexibility. Define your objectives, your resources and your deadlines. Anticipate possible obstacles, possible solutions and possible improvements.

Execute your projects with dedication, quality and originality. Do what you have to do, do it well and do it differently. Seek excellence, innovation and differentiation.

Evaluate your projects with honesty, humility and openness. Acknowledge your achievements, your mistakes and your learning. Appreciate your effort, your help and your feedback. Seek growth, improvement and collaboration.

In this chapter we have seen how we can harness our creativity and passion with optimism and resilience. We have learned what creativity and passion are and how they enhance our motivation and satisfaction. We have discovered how to discover our talent, our calling and our purpose. And we explored how to express our creativity and passion in our personal and professional projects.

To mis-step, to harness our creativity and our passion as a part of life. It involves using our imagination, our intuition and our divergent thinking. It means having a vocation, a purpose or a dream. It implies dedicating ourselves to what we like, to what makes us happy, to what gives us meaning.

If you apply what you have learned in this chapter, you will see how you feel more capable, more confident, more satisfied. You will see how you become more creative and more passionate.

Suggestion:

Cultivate your curiosity. Curiosity is the engine of creativity and passion. It makes you explore, investigate, discover new things. It makes you wonder, question, learn new things. It makes you attentive, receptive, surprised by things.

Find your inspiration. Inspiration is the fuel of creativity and passion. It makes you feel, imagine, create new things. It makes you connect, express, share new things. It makes you excited, enthusiastic, motivated about things.

Break your routine. Routine is the enemy of creativity and passion. It makes you get bored, stagnant, repeat the same things. It makes you disconnect, isolate yourself, ignore new things. It makes you tired, discouraged, dissatisfied with things.

Get out of your comfort zone. The comfort zone is the limit of creativity and passion. It makes you feel safe, comfortable, at ease with what you already know or do. It makes you avoid risk, challenge, change. It makes you conformist, mediocre, indifferent to things.

Face your fears. Fears are the obstacles to creativity and passion. They make you doubt, fear, paralyze you in the face of what you don't know or don't do. They make you reject opportunity, solution, innovation. They make you anxious, insecure, frustrated with things.

Experiment with different options. Options are the possibilities of creativity and passion. They make you try, vary, combine different things. They make you generate alternatives, solutions, improvements. They make you be open, flexible, original with things.

Learn from your mistakes. Mistakes are the masters of creativity and passion. They make you fail, make you wrong, correct what you do or know. They make you improve your skill, your knowledge, your competence. They make you humble, willing, persevering with things.

Collaborate with other people. People are the allies of creativity and passion. They accompany you, help you, support you in what you do or know. They make you contribute ideas, opinions, feedback. They make you be connected, respectful, collaborative with things.

Enjoy the process and the result. Enjoyment is the reward of creativity and passion. It makes you enjoy, have fun, rejoice in what you do or know. It makes you value your effort, your result, your impact. It makes you satisfied, proud, happy with things.

Share your creativity and passion with the world. Sharing is the purpose of creativity and passion. It makes you show, teach, offer what you do or know to the world. It makes you contribute to the well-being, to the development, to the progress of the world. It makes you generous, useful, transcendent with things.

Conclusion

Remember that the wrong step is to make the most of your creativity and your passion as part of life.

It involves using your imagination, intuition and divergent thinking.

It implies having a vocation, a purpose or a dream.

It involves dedicating yourself to what you like, to what makes you happy, to what gives you meaning.

If you apply these tips, you will see how you feel more capable, more confident, more satisfied.

You will see how you become a more creative and passionate person.

9. How to set realistic and achievable goals.

Goals are the objectives or purposes we set out to achieve in our personal or professional life. Goals help us to orient our action, to measure our progress, to evaluate our result. Goals are essential to make the wrong step go faster.

But not all goals are the same. There are goals that are realistic and achievable, and others that are not. Realistic and achievable goals are those that fit our reality, our capabilities and our circumstances. Goals that are not are those that are far from our reality, that exceed our capabilities or that ignore our circumstances.

Realistic and achievable goals are important for success because they allow us to move forward with confidence, motivation and satisfaction. They allow us to achieve what we set out to do without getting frustrated, giving up or being disappointed.

To set realistic and achievable goals we need to use the SMART method. The SMART method is a tool that helps us define our goals in a specific, measurable, achievable, relevant and time-bound manner. And we need to plan, execute and evaluate our goals effectively.

- What are realistic and achievable goals and why are they important for success?

Realistic and achievable goals are those that meet the following characteristics:

They are specific: they clearly and precisely define what we want to achieve, without ambiguities or generalities.

They are measurable: they establish criteria and indicators that allow us to check whether or not we have achieved our goal, and to what degree.

They are achievable: they fit our reality, our capabilities and our circumstances, without being too easy or too difficult.

They are relevant: they make sense for us, for our purpose or for our benefit, without being trivial or irrelevant.

They are temporary: they set a deadline or deadline for achieving our goal, neither too short nor too long.

Realistic and achievable goals are important for success because they offer the following advantages:

They orient us: they give us a direction, a course, a destination to go to.

They motivate us: they generate a desire, an interest, a commitment to achieve our goal.

They organize us: they facilitate the planning, execution and evaluation of our actions.

They challenge us: they stimulate us to get out of our comfort zone, to overcome our limits, to grow.

They satisfy us: they produce a pleasure, a joy, a pride in achieving our goal.

- How to use the SMART method to define your goals.

The SMART method is a tool that helps us define our goals in a specific, measurable, achievable, relevant and time-bound manner. To use the SMART method we can follow these steps:

Identify your overall goal: think about what you want to achieve in your personal or professional life, your dream or your purpose.

Divide your overall goal into subgoals: think of the steps or stages you need to accomplish to achieve your overall goal, intermediate or partial objectives.

Apply the SMART method to each sub-goal: think about how you can make each sub-goal more specific, more measurable, more achievable, more relevant and more time-bound.

Write your SMART sub-goals: formulate each sub-goal in a clear, concise and positive sentence that includes the elements of the SMART method.

Review your SMART subgoals: check if your subgoals meet the SMART criteria and if they are aligned with your overall goal.

For example:

Overall goal: I want to write a book about overcoming life's obstacles with optimism and resilience.

Subgoals:

Define the title, theme and target audience of the book.

Do a bibliographic research on the topic of the book.

Elaborate the table of contents and content of each chapter of the book.

Write the first draft of the book.

Review and proofread the first draft of the book.

Find a publisher or a platform to publish the book.

Promote and disseminate the book.

SMART Subgoals:

Define the title, theme and target audience of the book within one week, consulting with experts or people interested in the subject.

Do a bibliographic research on the topic of the book within one month, collecting at least 20 relevant and current sources of information.

Prepare the table of contents and content of each chapter of the book within two months, following a logical, coherent and attractive structure.

Write the first draft of the book within three months, writing at least 10 pages per day, in a clear, simple and entertaining style.

Revise and correct the first draft of the book within one month, soliciting the opinion and feedback of at least three trusted people.

Search for a publisher or a platform to publish the book within two months, contacting at least five different options and comparing their conditions and advantages.

Promote and disseminate the book within three months by creating a website, a social network and a blog about the book and participating in events, interviews and reviews related to the topic.

- How to plan, execute and evaluate your goals.

To plan, execute and evaluate your goals you can follow these tips:

Plan your goals in advance, in detail and with flexibility. Establish the steps, actions and resources you need to achieve your goals. Anticipate possible obstacles, possible solutions and possible improvements. Adapt your plan to the circumstances that arise.

Execute your goals with dedication, quality and originality. Do what you have to do, do it well and do it differently. Seek excellence, innovation and differentiation. Meet the deadlines, criteria and indicators you have set for yourself.

Evaluate your goals with honesty, humility and openness. Acknowledge your achievements, your mistakes and your learning. Appreciate your effort, your help and your feedback. Seek growth, improvement and collaboration.

In this chapter we have seen how we can set realistic and achievable goals with optimism and resilience. We have learned what realistic and achievable goals are and why they are important for success. We have discovered how to use the SMART method to define our goals. And we have explored how to plan, execute and evaluate our goals.

To take the wrong step in a hurry implies setting realistic and achievable goals as part of life. It implies orienting our action, measuring our progress, evaluating our result. It implies moving forward with confidence, motivation and satisfaction.

If you apply what you have learned in this chapter, you will see how you feel more capable, more confident, more satisfied. You will see how you become a more successful person.

Suggestion:

Define your goals clearly and precisely. Use the SMART method to make your goals specific, measurable, achievable, relevant and time-bound. Avoid ambiguous, vague or unrealistic goals.

Choose your goals with meaning and purpose. Make sure your goals are aligned with your vision, mission and values. Avoid goals that don't matter to you, don't engage you, or don't identify with you.

Break your goals into smaller, more manageable subgoals. Establish the steps or stages you need to accomplish to achieve your goals. Avoid goals that are too big, too complex or too far away.

Prioritize your goals according to their importance and urgency. Order your goals according to their relevance, benefit and timeframe. Avoid goals that are trivial, irrelevant or unnecessary.

Allocate the necessary resources to achieve your goals. Determine the time, money, material and people you need to achieve your goals. Avoid goals that are inaccessible, unfeasible or unsustainable.

Anticipate possible obstacles that may prevent you from achieving your goals. Identify the risks, difficulties and threats that may come your way. Avoid goals that are impossible, unwise or dangerous.

Seek the support of people who love and value you to achieve your goals. Share your goals with your family, your friends, your peers or your mentor. Ask for their advice, help, opinion or feedback. Thank them for their presence, their trust, their collaboration.

Execute your goals with dedication, quality and originality. Do what you have to do, do it well and do it differently. Seek excellence, innovation and differentiation in your actions. Meet the deadlines, criteria and indicators you have set for yourself.

Evaluate your goals with honesty, humility and openness. Acknowledge your achievements, your mistakes and your learning in the process of achieving your goals. Be grateful for your effort, your result, your impact. Look for growth, improvement and collaboration in your evaluation.

Celebrate your goals with joy, pride and generosity. Enjoy the pleasure, satisfaction and happiness of achieving your goals. Share your success, recognition and gratitude with the people who have supported or benefited you.

Conclusion

Here are ten detailed tips for setting realistic and achievable goals with optimism and resilience.

Remember that to make the wrong move in a hurry implies setting realistic and achievable goals as a part of life.

It involves guiding your action, measuring your progress, evaluating your performance.

It involves moving forward with confidence, motivation and satisfaction.

If you apply these tips, you will see how you feel more capable, more confident, more satisfied.

You will see how you become a more successful person.

10. How to celebrate your achievements and recognize your strengths.

Achievements and strengths are two aspects that make us feel proud, that make us value ourselves, that make us grow. Achievements and strengths are sources of self-knowledge and self-esteem. Achievements and strengths are essential ingredients to make the wrong step go faster.

Achievements are the results or successes we obtain by accomplishing our goals or our purposes. Achievements imply having done something well, having overcome a challenge, having contributed value.

Strengths are the qualities or capabilities we possess that make us stand out or differentiate us. Strengths imply having something good, having a talent, having a virtue.

To celebrate our achievements and recognize our strengths we need to be aware of them, without becoming arrogant or complacent. We need to know what we have done well, what we are good at and what we can do better. And we need to share our accomplishments and our strengths with others and be grateful for their support.

- What are achievements and strengths and why are they essential for self-knowledge?

Achievements and strengths are essential for self-knowledge because they allow us to know ourselves better, our capabilities, our values, our purposes. Self-knowledge is the process of discovering, understanding and accepting who we are, what we want and what we can do.

Achievements let us know our potential, our performance, our impact. They let us know what we are capable of, what we have achieved and what we have contributed.

Strengths allow us to know our abilities, our talents, our virtues. They allow us to know what we are good at, what differentiates us and what enriches us.

Self-knowledge is important because it helps us to:

Increase our self-esteem: by recognizing our achievements and strengths we feel more confident, more satisfied, more proud of ourselves.

Improve our self-efficacy: by recognizing our achievements and strengths we feel more capable, more competent, more prepared to face new challenges.

Develop our authenticity: by recognizing our achievements and strengths we feel more faithful, more coherent, more congruent with ourselves.

- How to recognize your achievements and strengths without becoming arrogant or complacent.

To recognize our achievements and strengths without becoming arrogant or complacent, we can follow these tips:

Be honest with yourself. Recognize your achievements and strengths objectively, without exaggerating or minimizing what you have done or what you have. Don't give yourself credit where credit is not due or deny yourself credit where credit is due.

Be humble with others. Recognize your achievements and strengths with modesty, without boasting or bragging about what you have done or what you have. Do not compare or compete with others or think yourself superior or inferior to them.

Be grateful for life. Acknowledge your achievements and strengths with gratitude, without taking them for granted or forgetting them. Don't settle for what you have done or what you have, but value what you have received and what you have to offer.

Be critical of yourself. Recognize your achievements and strengths with perspective, without being stagnant or satisfied with what you have done or what you have. Don't forget your mistakes or weaknesses but learn from them and improve them.

- How to share your accomplishments and strengths with others and thank them for their support.

To share our achievements and strengths with others and to thank them for their support, we can follow these tips:

Communicate your accomplishments and strengths clearly, simply and naturally. Explain what you have done, how you have done it and why you have done it. Express what you have, how you use it and what you use it for.

Celebrate your achievements and strengths with joy, pride and generosity. Enjoy the pleasure, satisfaction and happiness of having achieved or having something. Share your success, recognition and gratitude with the people who have supported or benefited you.

Use your achievements and strengths with responsibility, commitment and solidarity. Use what you have achieved or what you have to contribute to a greater good, to help other people, to improve the world.

In this chapter we have seen how we can celebrate our achievements and recognize our strengths with optimism and resilience. We have learned what achievements and strengths are and why they are essential for self-knowledge. We have discovered how to recognize our accomplishments and strengths without becoming arrogant or complacent. And we have explored how to share our accomplishments and strengths with others and be grateful for their support.

To misstep, to hustle involves celebrating our achievements and recognizing our strengths as part of life. It implies knowing our potential, our performance, our impact. It implies knowing our abilities, our talents, our virtues. It implies valuing, respecting and loving ourselves.

If you apply what you have learned in this chapter, you will see how you feel more confident, more satisfied, more proud. You will see how you become a more successful person.

Suggestion:

Keep track of your accomplishments and strengths. You can use a journal, a diary, an app, or any other method you like. Write down what you have achieved, what you have learned, what you have improved, what you liked, what made you proud or happy. Also write down the strengths you have used or developed, such as creativity, perseverance, communication, empathy, etc. This will help you have a more positive and realistic view of yourself and your potential.

Recognize the effort and process behind each achievement and strength. Don't just focus on the end result, but also on the road you have traveled to get there. Value the work, time, dedication, discipline, passion and will that you have put into each project or activity. This will help you appreciate more what you have achieved and develop a growth mindset.

Celebrate your accomplishments and strengths appropriately and proportionately. Don't settle for a simple "well done" or "I did it," but look for ways to reward yourself and enjoy your success. You can do something you enjoy, such as going to the movies, eating something tasty, buying something you want, etc. You can also share your joy with the people you care about, such as your family, your friends, your colleagues, etc. Just don't exaggerate or become arrogant or conceited. Remember that there is always room for improvement and that you are no better or worse than anyone else.

Be grateful for the support and help you have received from others. Recognize that you have not achieved everything alone, but that you have had the support and collaboration of others. Express your gratitude to those who have accompanied, advised, taught, inspired or motivated you along the way. You can do this verbally, in writing or gesturally. You can also return the favor or do something nice for them.

This will help you strengthen your relationships and create a climate of trust and reciprocity.

Compare your accomplishments and strengths to your own standards and goals. Don't compare yourself to others or what they do or have. Everyone has their own pace, their own level and their own story. The important thing is to be consistent with your vision, your mission and your values. Measure your progress and performance against your personal and professional goals. This will help you be more authentic and avoid envy or frustration.

Seek constructive and honest feedback from others. Don't settle for flattery or superficial or self-serving criticism. Seek the opinions of people who know you well, respect you and want your well-being. Listen to what they have to say about your accomplishments and strengths, both positive and negative. Accept feedback with humility and openness, without taking it as an attack or personal offense. This will help you improve your self-knowledge and correct your mistakes or weaknesses.

Share your accomplishments and strengths for educational or inspirational purposes. Don't use them to brag or to compete with others. Use your experience and knowledge to teach, mentor or help others who may be in a similar situation to you or who want to achieve similar goals as you. Be generous and supportive of what you know and what you can do. This will help you make a positive impact on the world and help you feel more useful and valuable.

Seek new challenges and opportunities to keep growing and learning. Don't stay stuck in your comfort zone or your past achievements. Look for ways to broaden your horizons, explore new fields, acquire new skills or improve existing ones. Set realistic but challenging goals that motivate and excite you. Don't be afraid to step out of your routine, to try new things, to make mistakes or to fail. This will help you maintain your curiosity and passion for life.

Seek balance between your achievements and strengths and the other aspects of your life. Don't become obsessed or dedicate yourself exclusively to your work, your studies or your personal project. Remember that there are other areas that are also important, such as health, family, friends, leisure, rest, etc. Try to distribute your time, energy and attention equally and harmoniously among all areas of your life. This will help you to have a fuller and happier life.

Be aware that your accomplishments and strengths do not define your value as a person. Don't base your self-esteem or your identity only on what you do or what you can do. Remember that you are much more than that, that you have other qualities and characteristics that make you unique and special. Recognize and accept your virtues and your defects, your successes and your mistakes, your successes and your failures. Be true to yourself and your principles. This will help you to be more human and happier.

Conclusion: Celebrating your achievements and recognizing your strengths is a way of acknowledging your worth, appreciating your effort, enjoying your success and motivating you to move forward. However, you should not become arrogant or complacent, but rather maintain a humble, grateful, generous and open attitude to learning. In this way you can continue to grow as a person and as a professional, and contribute to the welfare of others. I hope you find these tips useful and that you put them into practice in your life.

11. Conclusion.

You have reached the end of this book. I hope you have enjoyed reading it and that you have learned something new, useful and valuable. I hope that you have found in these pages support, inspiration and motivation to overcome life's obstacles with optimism and resilience.

In this book, we have seen that the bad step must be taken in haste, that is, we must act quickly and decisively in difficult situations, without being overcome by fear or despair. We have seen that we must take control of our lives, take responsibility for our actions and seek creative and effective solutions.

We have also seen that the right step must be taken in a hurry, that is, we must seize opportunities, celebrate achievements and recognize strengths. We have seen that we must have a clear vision and purpose to guide and motivate us. We have seen that we must develop confidence in ourselves and in our abilities.

We have seen, in short, that we must live with a positive attitude, with gratitude, with joy and with humor. We have seen that we must communicate effectively and create positive relationships. We have seen that we must learn from mistakes and failures. We have seen that we must adapt to change and uncertainty. We have seen to harness our creativity and passion. We have seen to set realistic and achievable goals.

But above all, we have seen that all this depends on us, on our will, on our effort, on our commitment. We have seen that we are the protagonists, the heroes or heroines of our own history. And we have seen that we can write that story as we wish, with our dreams, with our values, with our heart.

So I invite you to keep writing your story, to keep hurrying the bad step and the good step. I invite you to keep growing, to keep improving, to keep enjoying. I invite you to keep living.

Thank you very much for reading this wonderful book. I hope you have found it helpful and enjoyable. And I hope you keep in touch with me, because soon I will upload more personal growth content for you. Content that will make you reflect, feel and act. Content that will make you happier.

And remember: to the bad step give haste, to the good step also. Because life is a wonderful adventure, but also full of surprises, difficulties and opportunities. And you are the protagonist, the hero or heroine of your own story.

So don't wait any longer. Open your mind, open your heart, open your wings. And fly high, so high. To infinity and beyond.

A big hug,

Also by Santos Omar Medrano Chura

Aprende a escuchar las críticas. Cómo convertir los comentarios negativos en oportunidades de crecimiento.

La negación de lo desconocido. Cómo superar el miedo y la resistencia al cambio.

Learn to listen to criticism. How to turn negative comments into growth opportunities.

The denial of the unknown. How to overcome fear and resistance to change.

112 Consejos para fortalecer tu PACIENCIA y alcanzar tus metas

128 Consejos para el Mejoramiento Personal

Como ser un Buen Líder. Desarrolla el liderazgo para hacer una diferencia positiva en tu equipo y organización.

Desarrolla tu Inteligencia Emocional. Cómo entender y gestionar tus emociones para tener éxito en la vida.

Domina tu aprendizaje. Estrategias y técnicas efectivas para estudiar con éxito.

Elimina todo lo negativo de tu persona.

Aprendiendo a decir No sin sentir culpa o remordimiento. Cómo establecer límites saludables y tomar el control de tu vida.

El arte de la disciplina. Cómo lograr tus metas con hábitos saludables.

El mundo es tuyo. Cómo lograr tus sueños y vivir con plenitud.

El poder de la fuerza de voluntad. Cómo desarrollar hábitos positivos y alcanzar tus metas.

El secreto del ahora. Cómo vivir plenamente y sin estrés con la sabiduría del presente.

La mente resiliente. Cómo superar los obstáculos y los desafíos.

Mejoramiento del Cerebro. Cómo optimizar tu cerebro para una vida más plena.

Supera tu timidez.

Cómo anticiparse al futuro.

Como ser puntual. El arte de llegar a tiempo a todo.

El Poder de la Decisión. Desbloquea tu Potencial y Crea el Futuro que Deseas.

La Guía Definitiva para Criar Hijos Exitosos.

La mente ganadora. Cómo desarrollar el pensamiento de la gente exitosa.

La suerte no existe. Cómo crear tu propio destino con inteligencia y acción.

Mañana será otro día. Cómo afrontar los desafíos de la vida con optimismo.

Nunca Te Rindas 2. 76 consejos para alcanzar tus sueños sin rendirte.

Piensa como un triunfador. Los secretos de la psicología del éxito.

Vive la vida con optimismo.

Aléjate del hombre tóxico. Cómo liberarte de una relación destructiva y recuperar tu autoestima.

Al mal paso darle prisa.

Al mal tiempo, buena cara. Cómo encontrar la felicidad en las dificultades.

A palabras necias, oídos sordos.

Crisis Oportunidad. Cómo transformar los desafíos en éxitos.

Dime qué comes y te diré quién eres.

El poder de la positividad. Cómo rodearte de personas que te inspiran y te motivan.

El poder de las relaciones. Cómo elegir a las personas que te ayudan a crecer y a alcanzar tus metas.

El tiempo es oro. Cómo transformar tu vida con el poder del tiempo.

Gatitos felices. Todo lo que necesitas saber para cuidar a tu pequeño amigo.

Hazlo ya. Cómo dejar de procrastinar y cumplir tus sueños.

La luz al final del túnel. Cómo vencer la depresión y recuperar la alegría de vivir.

Libérate de la mujer tóxica. Cómo salir de una relación dañina y reconstruir tu felicidad.

No te culpes, actúa.

Pedalea hacia tus sueños. Cómo el ciclismo te ayuda a superar los obstáculos y alcanzar tus metas.

Planeta en peligro. Cómo proteger nuestro hogar común para las generaciones venideras.

Siempre listos. Cómo prepararse para cualquier situación y superar los desafíos de la vida.

Supera el miedo y abraza las oportunidades.

Tu sueño hecho realidad. Cómo transformar tu vida con el poder de tu mente.

Vencer al miedo. Estrategias prácticas para superar tus temores y alcanzar tus metas.

Vive en paz. Cómo sanar tu mente y tu corazón con la conciencia tranquila.

112 Tips to strengthen your patience and achieve your goals.

128 Tips for Personal Improvement. Set clear and achievable goals.

Develop Your Emotional Intelligence.

Eliminate everything negative about your person.

How to Be a Good Leader. Develop leadership to make a positive difference in your team and organization.

Master your learning. Effective strategies and techniques for successful study.

How to anticipate the future. Strategies and tips to be prepared for any situation.

Live life with optimism.

How to be punctual. The art of being on time for everything.

Overcome Fear and Embrace Opportunities.

There is no Such Thing as Luck.

Always ready. How to prepare for any situation and overcome life's challenges.
The Definitive Guide to Raising Successful Children.
The Power of Positivity.
Do It Now. How to stop procrastinating and fulfill your dreams.
Don't Blame Yourself, Act.
Free Yourself from Toxic Women
Happy Kittens. Everything You Need to Know to Take Care of Your Little Friend.
Stay Away from the Toxic Man.
The Time Is Gold. How to transform your life with the power of time.
To Bad Weather, Good Face. How to find happiness in difficulties.
To the Bad Step, Give Haste.

Milton Keynes UK
Ingram Content Group UK Ltd.
UKHW041821211123
432980UK00001BB/100